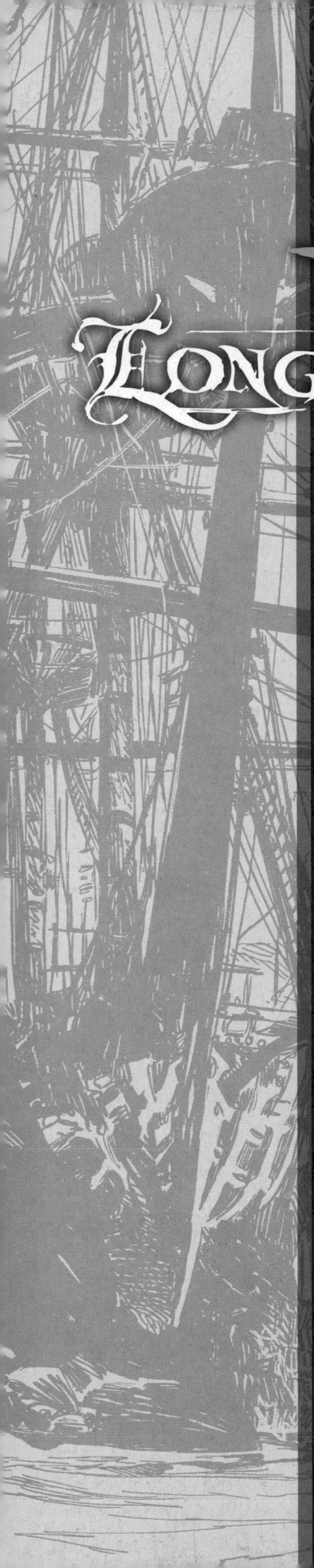

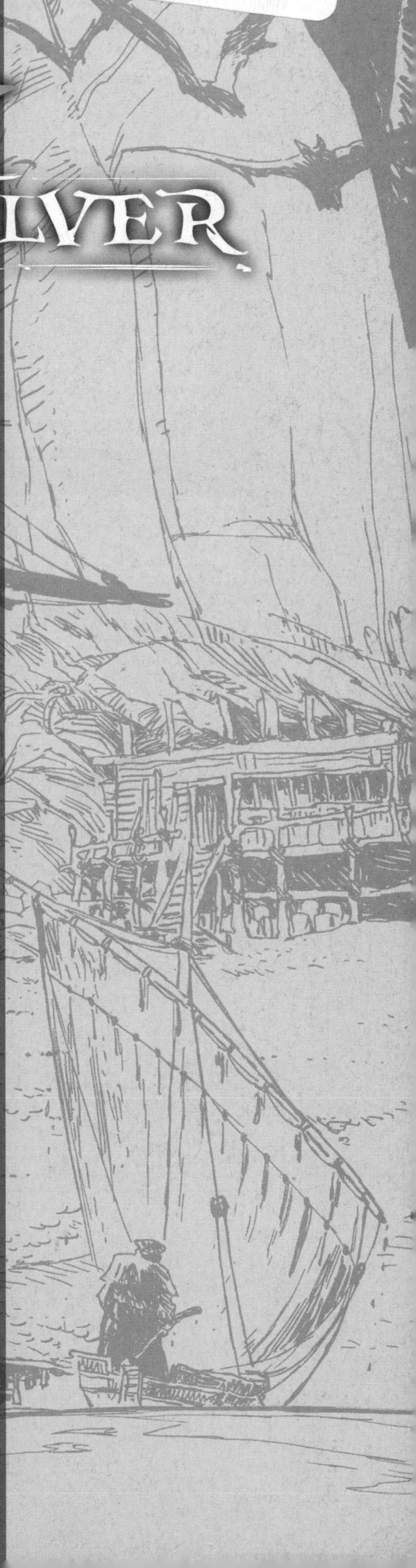

# Long John Silver

## I - Lady Vivian Hastings

Xavier
Dorison

Mathieu
Lauffray

Original title: Long John Silver 1 – Lady Vivian Hastings
Original edition: © Dargaud Paris, 2007 by Dorison & Lauffray
www.dargaud.com - All rights reserved
English translation: © 2010 Cinebook Ltd
Translator: Jerome Saincantin
Lettering and text layout: Imadjinn
Printed in Spain by Just Colour Graphic
This edition first published in Great Britain in 2010 by
Cinebook Ltd - 56 Beech Avenue
Canterbury, Kent - CT4 7TA
www.cinebook.com
A CIP catalogue record for this book
is available from the British Library
ISBN 978-1-84918-062-7

9th CINEBOOK
The 9th Art Publisher

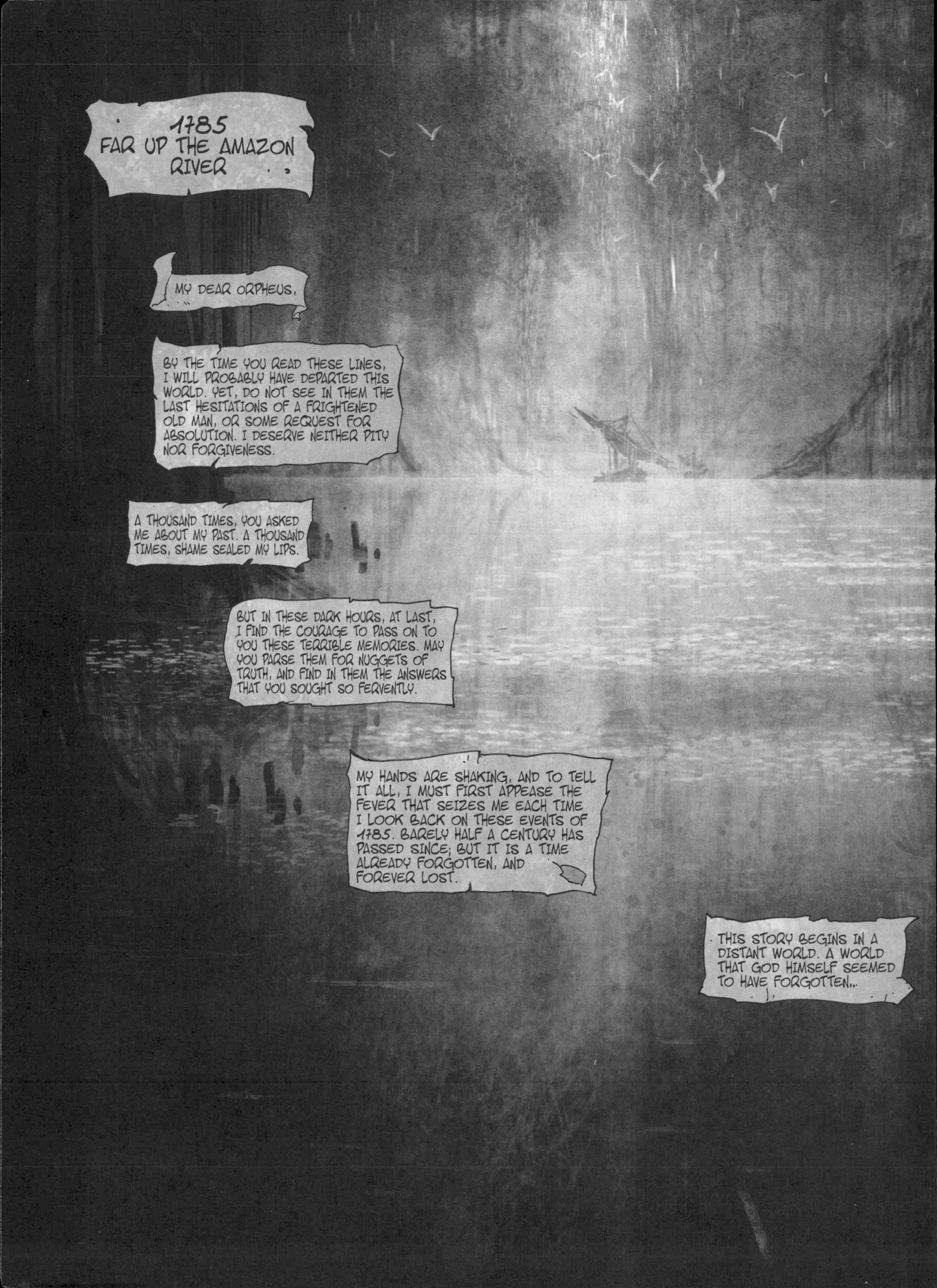
1785
FAR UP THE AMAZON RIVER
MY DEAR ORPHEUS,
BY THE TIME YOU READ THESE LINES, I WILL PROBABLY HAVE DEPARTED THIS WORLD. YET, DO NOT SEE IN THEM THE LAST HESITATIONS OF A FRIGHTENED OLD MAN, OR SOME REQUEST FOR ABSOLUTION. I DESERVE NEITHER PITY NOR FORGIVENESS.
A THOUSAND TIMES, YOU ASKED ME ABOUT MY PAST. A THOUSAND TIMES, SHAME SEALED MY LIPS.
BUT IN THESE DARK HOURS, AT LAST, I FIND THE COURAGE TO PASS ON TO YOU THESE TERRIBLE MEMORIES. MAY YOU PARSE THEM FOR NUGGETS OF TRUTH, AND FIND IN THEM THE ANSWERS THAT YOU SOUGHT SO FERVENTLY.
MY HANDS ARE SHAKING, AND TO TELL IT ALL, I MUST FIRST APPEASE THE FEVER THAT SEIZES ME EACH TIME I LOOK BACK ON THESE EVENTS OF 1785. BARELY HALF A CENTURY HAS PASSED SINCE; BUT IT IS A TIME ALREADY FORGOTTEN, AND FOREVER LOST.
THIS STORY BEGINS IN A DISTANT WORLD. A WORLD THAT GOD HIMSELF SEEMED TO HAVE FORGOTTEN...

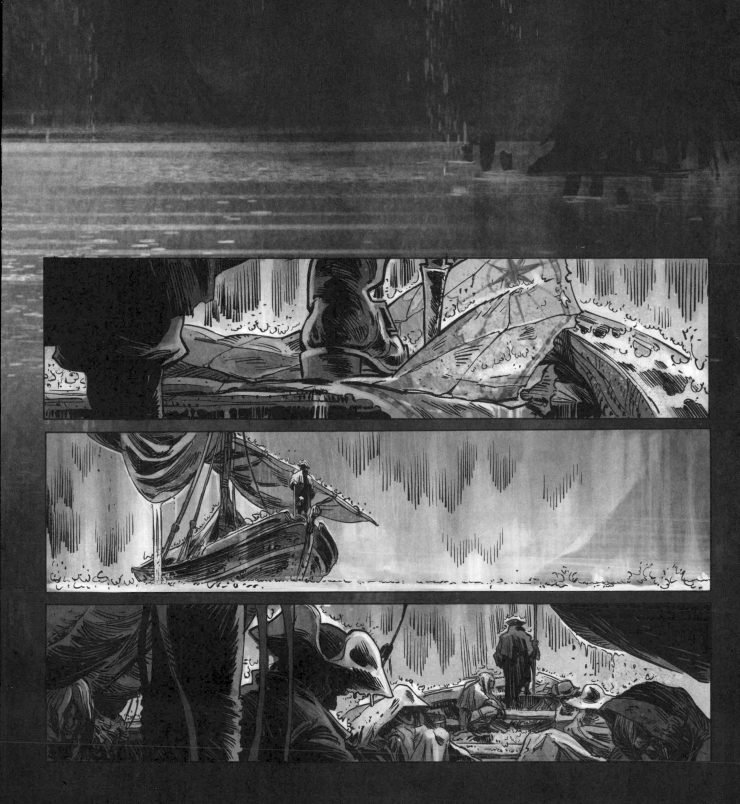

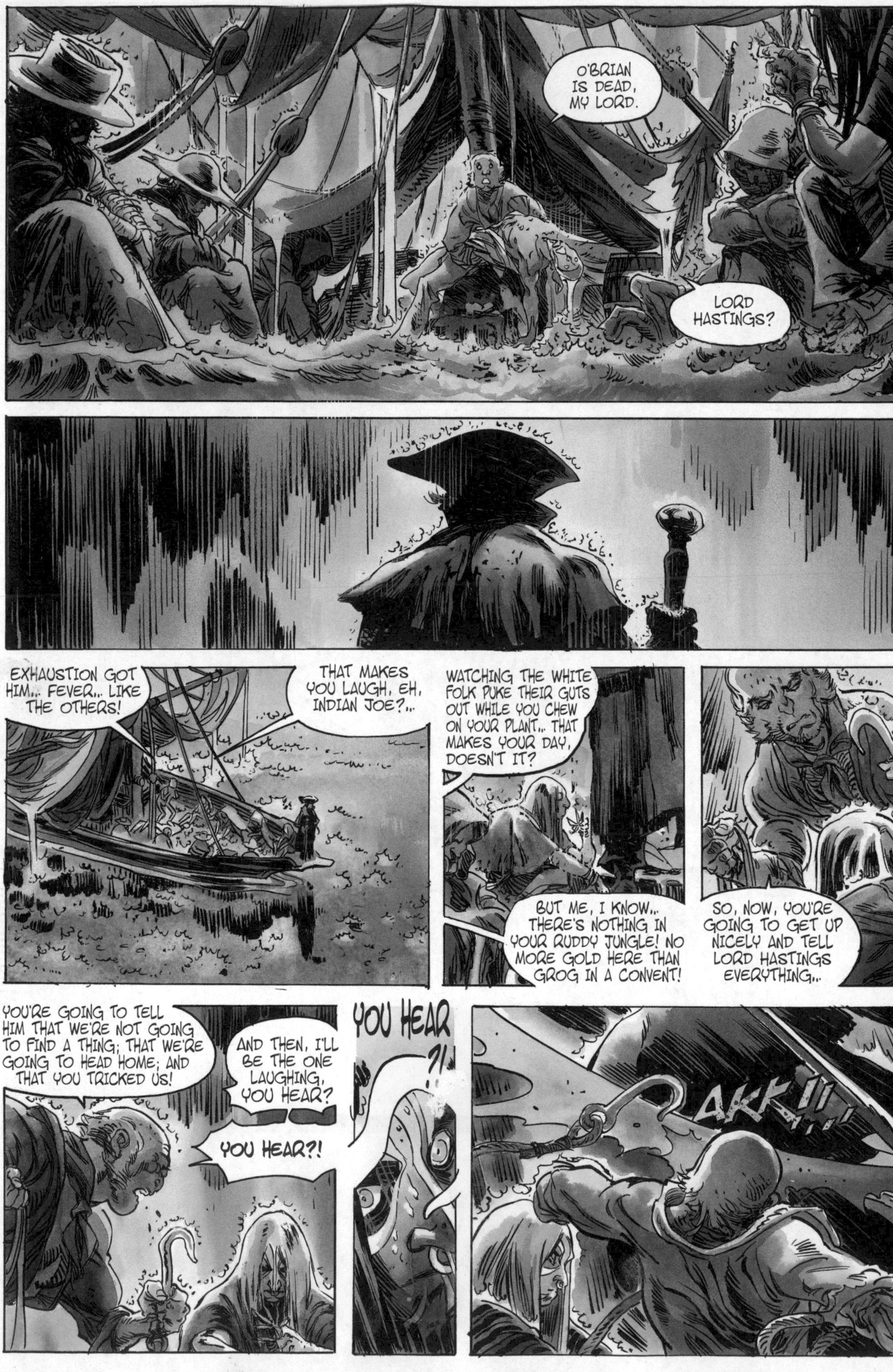
O'BRIAN IS DEAD, MY LORD.
LORD HASTINGS?
EXHAUSTION GOT HIM... FEVER... LIKE THE OTHERS!
THAT MAKES YOU LAUGH, EH, INDIAN JOE?...
WATCHING THE WHITE FOLK PUKE THEIR GUTS OUT WHILE YOU CHEW ON YOUR PLANT... THAT MAKES YOUR DAY, DOESN'T IT?
BUT ME, I KNOW... THERE'S NOTHING IN YOUR RUDDY JUNGLE! NO MORE GOLD HERE THAN GROG IN A CONVENT!
SO, NOW, YOU'RE GOING TO GET UP NICELY AND TELL LORD HASTINGS EVERYTHING...
YOU'RE GOING TO TELL HIM THAT WE'RE NOT GOING TO FIND A THING; THAT WE'RE GOING TO HEAD HOME; AND THAT YOU TRICKED US!
AND THEN, I'LL BE THE ONE LAUGHING, YOU HEAR?
YOU HEAR?!
YOU HEAR ?!
AKK!!..

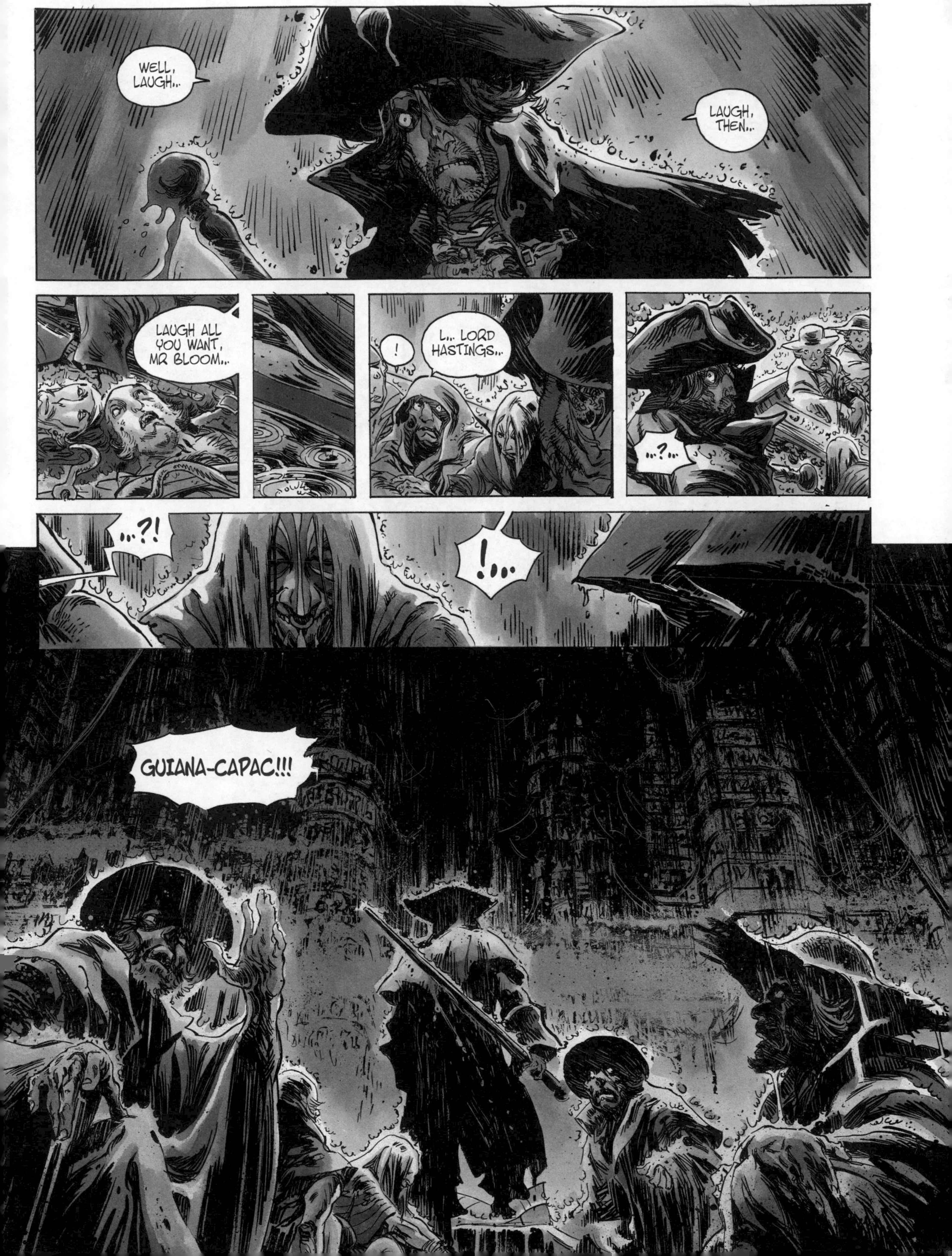

WELL, LAUGH...
LAUGH, THEN...
LAUGH ALL YOU WANT, MR BLOOM...
!
L... LORD HASTINGS...
...?...
...?!
!...
GUIANA-CAPAC!!!

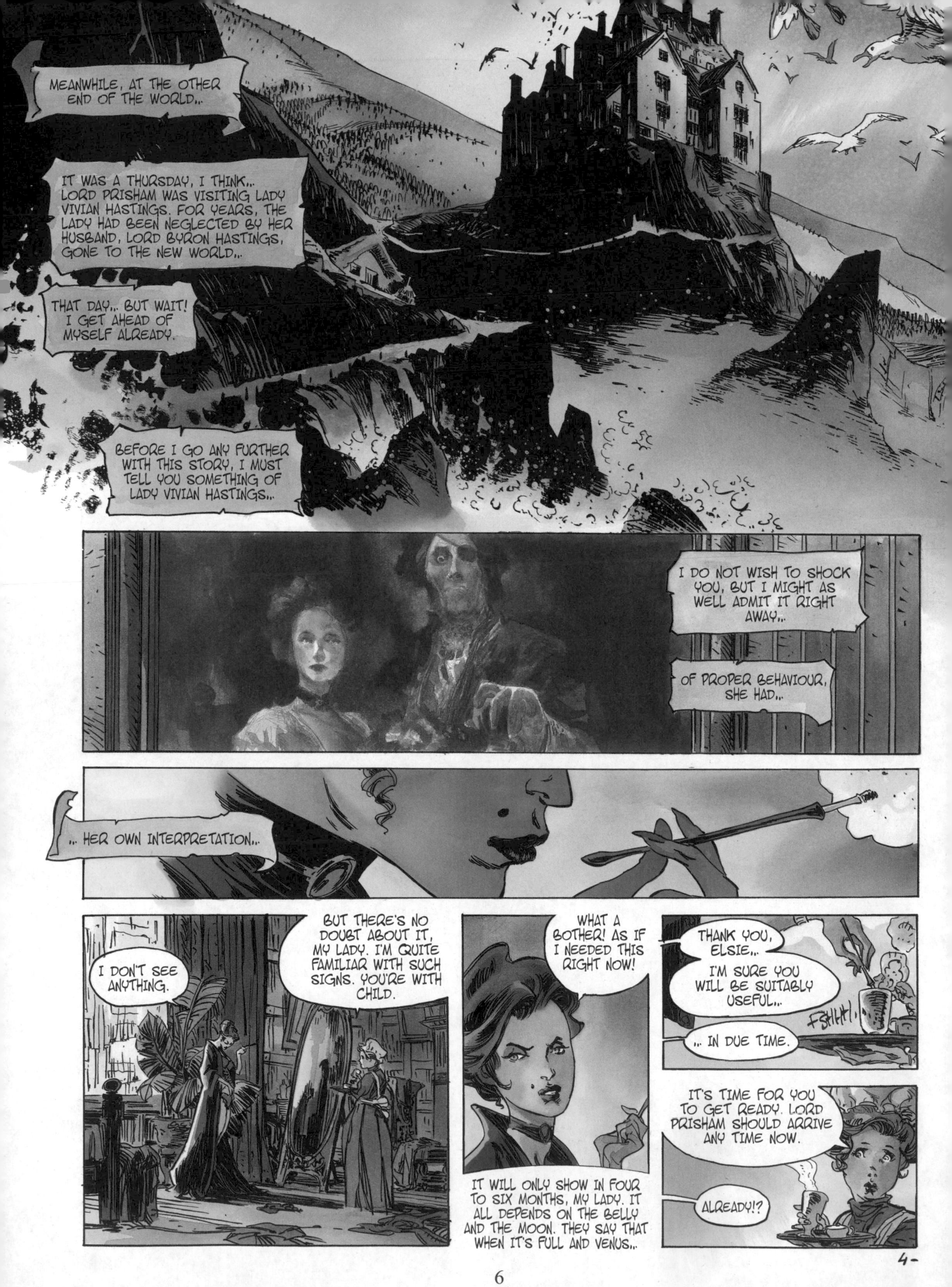
MEANWHILE, AT THE OTHER END OF THE WORLD...
IT WAS A THURSDAY, I THINK... LORD PRISHAM WAS VISITING LADY VIVIAN HASTINGS. FOR YEARS, THE LADY HAD BEEN NEGLECTED BY HER HUSBAND, LORD BYRON HASTINGS, GONE TO THE NEW WORLD...
THAT DAY... BUT WAIT! I GET AHEAD OF MYSELF ALREADY.
BEFORE I GO ANY FURTHER WITH THIS STORY, I MUST TELL YOU SOMETHING OF LADY VIVIAN HASTINGS...
I DO NOT WISH TO SHOCK YOU, BUT I MIGHT AS WELL ADMIT IT RIGHT AWAY...
OF PROPER BEHAVIOUR, SHE HAD...
... HER OWN INTERPRETATION...
I DON'T SEE ANYTHING.
BUT THERE'S NO DOUBT ABOUT IT, MY LADY. I'M QUITE FAMILIAR WITH SUCH SIGNS. YOU'RE WITH CHILD.
WHAT A BOTHER! AS IF I NEEDED THIS RIGHT NOW!
IT WILL ONLY SHOW IN FOUR TO SIX MONTHS, MY LADY. IT ALL DEPENDS ON THE BELLY AND THE MOON. THEY SAY THAT WHEN IT'S FULL AND VENUS...
THANK YOU, ELSIE...
I'M SURE YOU WILL BE SUITABLY USEFUL...
FSHHH!
... IN DUE TIME.
IT'S TIME FOR YOU TO GET READY. LORD PRISHAM SHOULD ARRIVE ANY TIME NOW.
ALREADY!?
4-

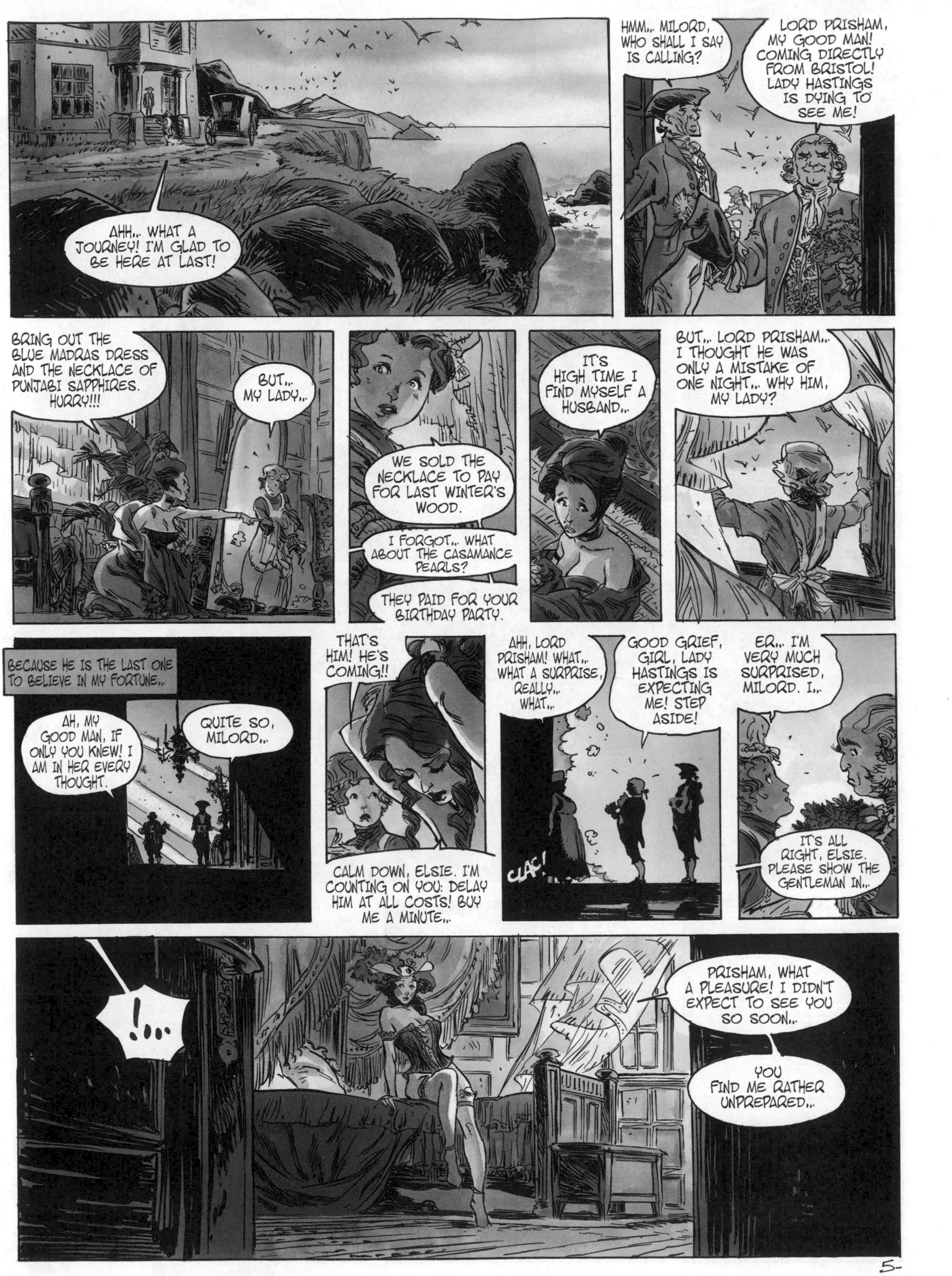
AHH... WHAT A JOURNEY! I'M GLAD TO BE HERE AT LAST!
HMM... MILORD, WHO SHALL I SAY IS CALLING?
LORD PRISHAM, MY GOOD MAN! COMING DIRECTLY FROM BRISTOL! LADY HASTINGS IS DYING TO SEE ME!
BRING OUT THE BLUE MADRAS DRESS AND THE NECKLACE OF PUNJABI SAPPHIRES. HURRY!!!
BUT... MY LADY...
WE SOLD THE NECKLACE TO PAY FOR LAST WINTER'S WOOD.
I FORGOT... WHAT ABOUT THE CASAMANCE PEARLS?
THEY PAID FOR YOUR BIRTHDAY PARTY.
IT'S HIGH TIME I FIND MYSELF A HUSBAND...
BUT... LORD PRISHAM... I THOUGHT HE WAS ONLY A MISTAKE OF ONE NIGHT... WHY HIM, MY LADY?
BECAUSE HE IS THE LAST ONE TO BELIEVE IN MY FORTUNE...
AH, MY GOOD MAN, IF ONLY YOU KNEW! I AM IN HER EVERY THOUGHT.
QUITE SO, MILORD...
THAT'S HIM! HE'S COMING!!
CALM DOWN, ELSIE. I'M COUNTING ON YOU: DELAY HIM AT ALL COSTS! BUY ME A MINUTE...
AHH, LORD PRISHAM! WHAT... WHAT A SURPRISE, REALLY... WHAT...
GOOD GRIEF, GIRL, LADY HASTINGS IS EXPECTING ME! STEP ASIDE!
CLAC!
ER... I'M VERY MUCH SURPRISED, MILORD. I...
IT'S ALL RIGHT, ELSIE. PLEASE SHOW THE GENTLEMAN IN...
!...
PRISHAM, WHAT A PLEASURE! I DIDN'T EXPECT TO SEE YOU SO SOON...
YOU FIND ME RATHER UNPREPARED...
5-

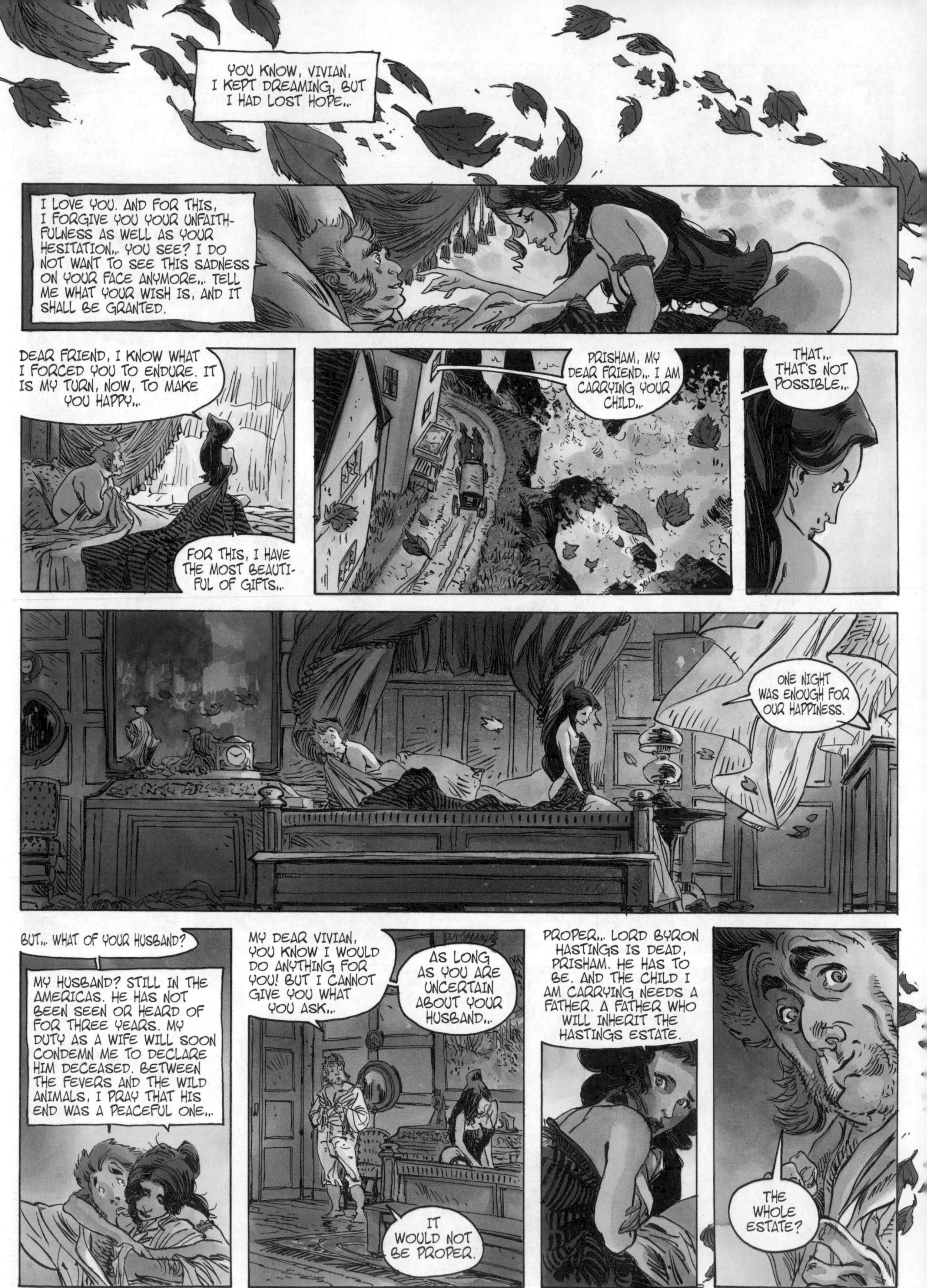

YOU KNOW, VIVIAN, I KEPT DREAMING, BUT I HAD LOST HOPE...
I LOVE YOU. AND FOR THIS, I FORGIVE YOU YOUR UNFAITH-FULNESS AS WELL AS YOUR HESITATION... YOU SEE? I DO NOT WANT TO SEE THIS SADNESS ON YOUR FACE ANYMORE... TELL ME WHAT YOUR WISH IS, AND IT SHALL BE GRANTED.
DEAR FRIEND, I KNOW WHAT I FORCED YOU TO ENDURE. IT IS MY TURN, NOW, TO MAKE YOU HAPPY...
FOR THIS, I HAVE THE MOST BEAUTI-FUL OF GIFTS...
PRISHAM, MY DEAR FRIEND... I AM CARRYING YOUR CHILD...
THAT... THAT'S NOT POSSIBLE...
ONE NIGHT WAS ENOUGH FOR OUR HAPPINESS.
BUT... WHAT OF YOUR HUSBAND?
MY HUSBAND? STILL IN THE AMERICAS. HE HAS NOT BEEN SEEN OR HEARD OF FOR THREE YEARS. MY DUTY AS A WIFE WILL SOON CONDEMN ME TO DECLARE HIM DECEASED. BETWEEN THE FEVERS AND THE WILD ANIMALS, I PRAY THAT HIS END WAS A PEACEFUL ONE...
MY DEAR VIVIAN, YOU KNOW I WOULD DO ANYTHING FOR YOU! BUT I CANNOT GIVE YOU WHAT YOU ASK...
AS LONG AS YOU ARE UNCERTAIN ABOUT YOUR HUSBAND...
IT WOULD NOT BE PROPER.
PROPER... LORD BYRON HASTINGS IS DEAD, PRISHAM. HE HAS TO BE. AND THE CHILD I AM CARRYING NEEDS A FATHER. A FATHER WHO WILL INHERIT THE HASTINGS ESTATE.
THE WHOLE ESTATE?

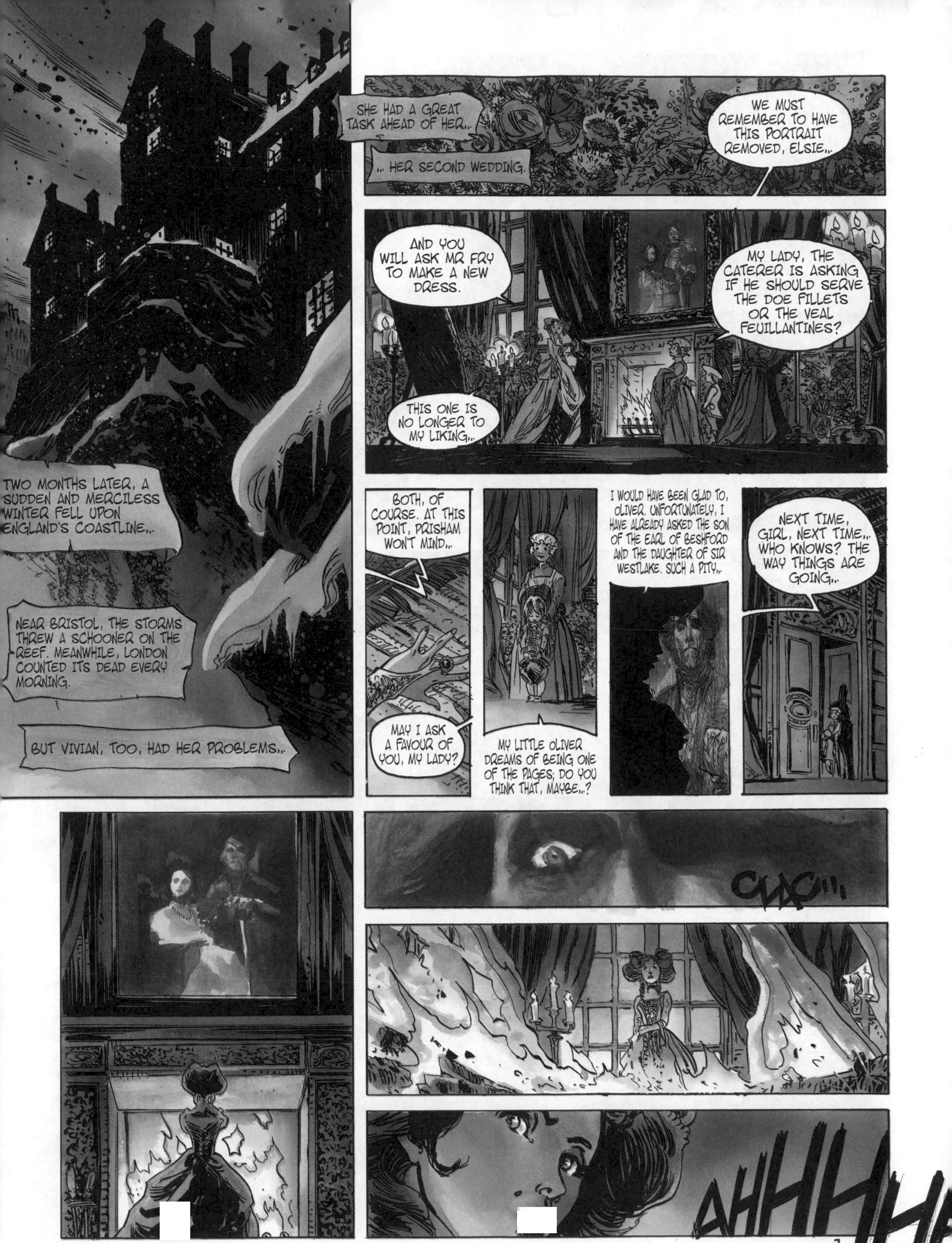

TWO MONTHS LATER, A SUDDEN AND MERCILESS WINTER FELL UPON ENGLAND'S COASTLINE...
NEAR BRISTOL, THE STORMS THREW A SCHOONER ON THE REEF. MEANWHILE, LONDON COUNTED ITS DEAD EVERY MORNING.
BUT VIVIAN, TOO, HAD HER PROBLEMS...
SHE HAD A GREAT TASK AHEAD OF HER...
... HER SECOND WEDDING.
WE MUST REMEMBER TO HAVE THIS PORTRAIT REMOVED, ELSIE...
AND YOU WILL ASK MR FRY TO MAKE A NEW DRESS.
THIS ONE IS NO LONGER TO MY LIKING...
MY LADY, THE CATERER IS ASKING IF HE SHOULD SERVE THE DOE FILLETS OR THE VEAL FEUILLANTINES?
BOTH, OF COURSE. AT THIS POINT, PRISHAM WON'T MIND...
MAY I ASK A FAVOUR OF YOU, MY LADY?
MY LITTLE OLIVER DREAMS OF BEING ONE OF THE PAGES; DO YOU THINK THAT, MAYBE...?
I WOULD HAVE BEEN GLAD TO, OLIVER. UNFORTUNATELY, I HAVE ALREADY ASKED THE SON OF THE EARL OF BESHFORD AND THE DAUGHTER OF SIR WESTLAKE. SUCH A PITY...
NEXT TIME, GIRL, NEXT TIME... WHO KNOWS? THE WAY THINGS ARE GOING...
CLAC!!
AHHHH
7-

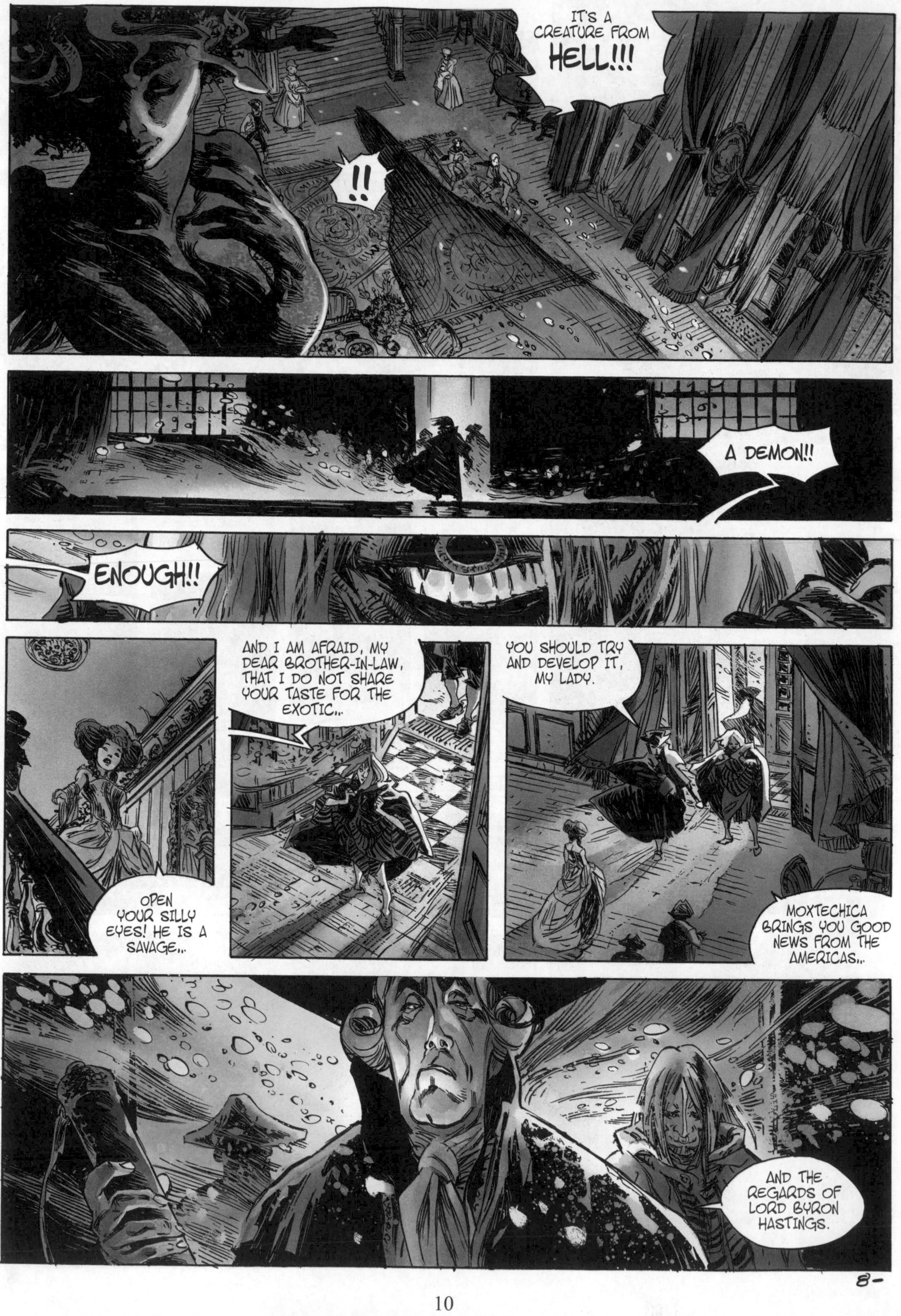
IT'S A CREATURE FROM HELL!!!
!!
A DEMON!!
ENOUGH!!
OPEN YOUR SILLY EYES! HE IS A SAVAGE...
AND I AM AFRAID, MY DEAR BROTHER-IN-LAW, THAT I DO NOT SHARE YOUR TASTE FOR THE EXOTIC...
YOU SHOULD TRY AND DEVELOP IT, MY LADY.
MOXTECHICA BRINGS YOU GOOD NEWS FROM THE AMERICAS...
AND THE REGARDS OF LORD BYRON HASTINGS.
8-

MOXTECHICA ARRIVED IN PORTSMOUTH A WEEK AGO. HE TRACKED ME DOWN A FEW DAYS LATER... I IMMEDIATELY REQUESTED A LEAVE OF ABSENCE TO COME SEE YOU...
A DELICIOUS MEAL, MY LADY.
WAS HIS MAJESTY'S NAVY NOT SUPPOSED TO SET SAIL AND HAVE AT IT ONCE MORE WITH OUR FRENCH FRIENDS?
IT WOULD HAVE BEEN MY SEVENTH CAMPAIGN, AND MY PROMOTION TO POST CAPTAIN. BUT YOUR HUSBAND ALSO HAPPENS TO BE MY BROTHER, AND HE HAD ME DELIVER HIS LETTER IN PERSON. WE HASTINGS PLACE DUTY TO OUR FAMILY AND THE CROWN BEFORE PERSONAL CONSIDERATIONS.
YES, CAPTAIN. WHAT AN ADMIRABLE FAMILY YOU ARE. ALL OF YOU, SO VERY... LIKE MY HUSBAND.
SO... THIS SAVAGE WAS WITH HIM IN THE AMERICAS...
DOES HE SPEAK OUR LANGUAGE?
A FEW WORDS. BUT HE UNDERSTANDS ALMOST EVERYTHING.
GOOD... WELL, THEN, MOXTE... MOTE... MOCHE... FINE. MOC. LET US SAY "MOC." WHAT GOOD NEWS DO YOU BRING FROM LORD BYRON? IS HE DOING WELL?
YES.
THIS IS HAPPY NEWS. HE IS IN GOOD HEALTH? HIS MEN ARE TAKING GOOD CARE OF HIM? WILD ANIMALS ARE LEAVING HIM ALONE?
YES.
I FEEL BETTER ALREADY. AND THIS LETTER HE HAS SENT ME—MAY I SEE IT AT LAST?
MY DEAR LADY HASTINGS, I WOULD PREFER TO APPRISE YOU OF ITS CONTENTS...
... IN PRIVATE.
9-

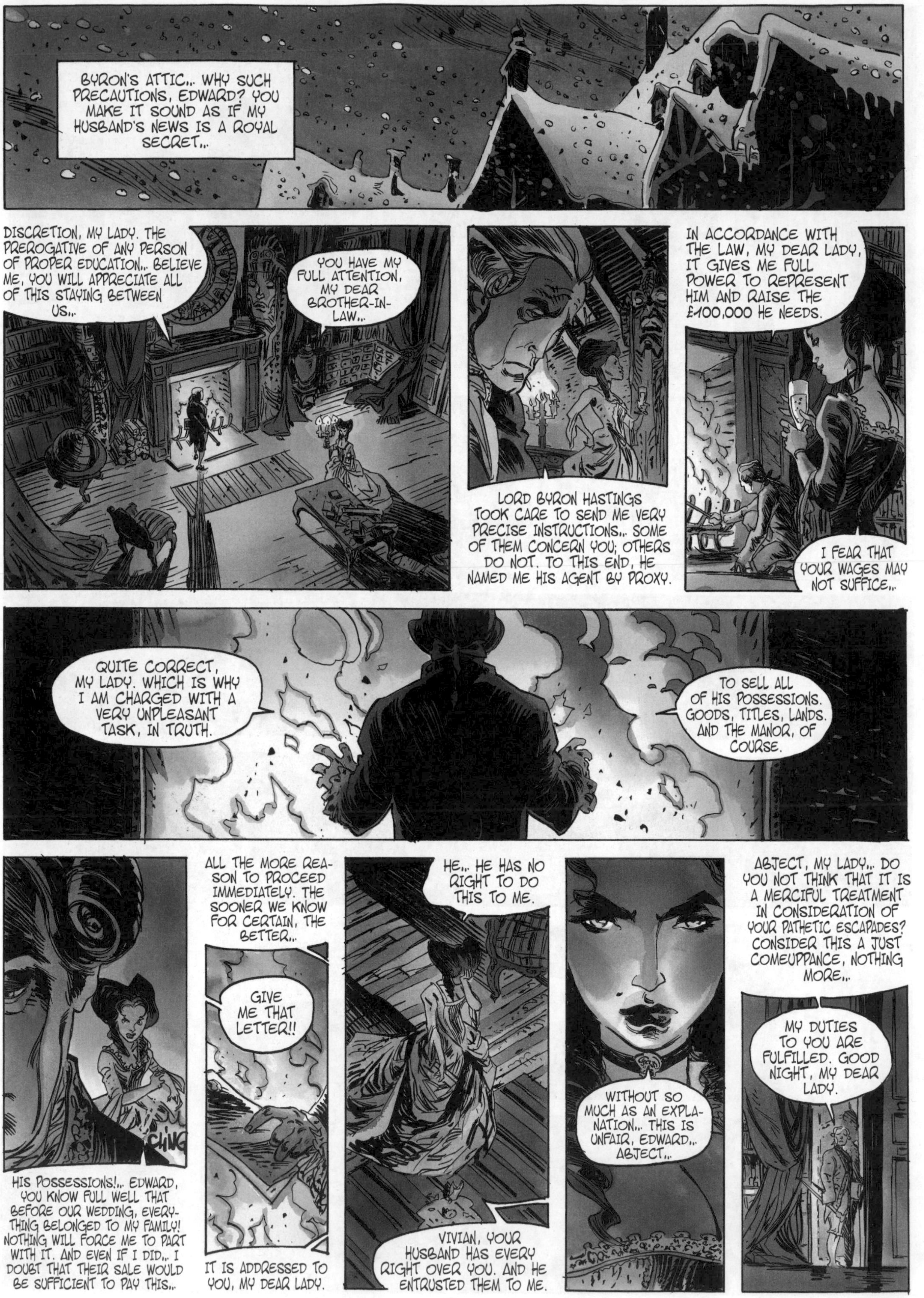

BYRON'S ATTIC,.. WHY SUCH PRECAUTIONS, EDWARD? YOU MAKE IT SOUND AS IF MY HUSBAND'S NEWS IS A ROYAL SECRET,..
DISCRETION, MY LADY. THE PREROGATIVE OF ANY PERSON OF PROPER EDUCATION,.. BELIEVE ME, YOU WILL APPRECIATE ALL OF THIS STAYING BETWEEN US,..
YOU HAVE MY FULL ATTENTION, MY DEAR BROTHER-IN-LAW,..
LORD BYRON HASTINGS TOOK CARE TO SEND ME VERY PRECISE INSTRUCTIONS,.. SOME OF THEM CONCERN YOU; OTHERS DO NOT. TO THIS END, HE NAMED ME HIS AGENT BY PROXY.
IN ACCORDANCE WITH THE LAW, MY DEAR LADY, IT GIVES ME FULL POWER TO REPRESENT HIM AND RAISE THE £100,000 HE NEEDS.
I FEAR THAT YOUR WAGES MAY NOT SUFFICE,..
QUITE CORRECT, MY LADY. WHICH IS WHY I AM CHARGED WITH A VERY UNPLEASANT TASK, IN TRUTH.
TO SELL ALL OF HIS POSSESSIONS. GOODS, TITLES, LANDS. AND THE MANOR, OF COURSE.
CHING
HIS POSSESSIONS!,.. EDWARD, YOU KNOW FULL WELL THAT BEFORE OUR WEDDING, EVERYTHING BELONGED TO MY FAMILY! NOTHING WILL FORCE ME TO PART WITH IT. AND EVEN IF I DID,.. I DOUBT THAT THEIR SALE WOULD BE SUFFICIENT TO PAY THIS,..
ALL THE MORE REASON TO PROCEED IMMEDIATELY. THE SOONER WE KNOW FOR CERTAIN, THE BETTER,..
GIVE ME THAT LETTER!!
IT IS ADDRESSED TO YOU, MY DEAR LADY.
HE,.. HE HAS NO RIGHT TO DO THIS TO ME.
VIVIAN, YOUR HUSBAND HAS EVERY RIGHT OVER YOU. AND HE ENTRUSTED THEM TO ME.
WITHOUT SO MUCH AS AN EXPLANATION,.. THIS IS UNFAIR, EDWARD,.. ABJECT,..
ABJECT, MY LADY,.. DO YOU NOT THINK THAT IT IS A MERCIFUL TREATMENT IN CONSIDERATION OF YOUR PATHETIC ESCAPADES? CONSIDER THIS A JUST COMEUPPANCE, NOTHING MORE,..
MY DUTIES TO YOU ARE FULFILLED. GOOD NIGHT, MY DEAR LADY.
10-

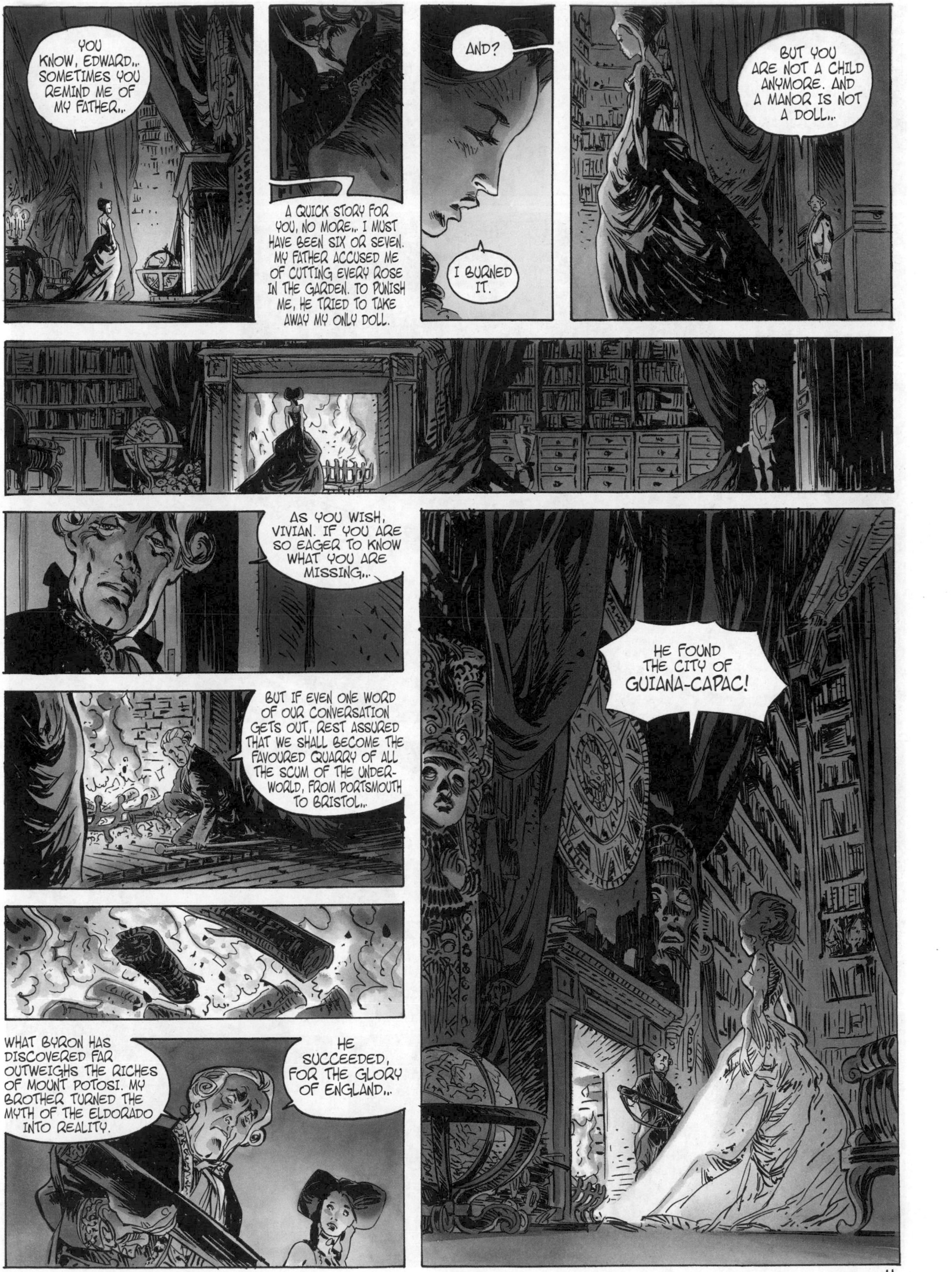
YOU KNOW, EDWARD... SOMETIMES YOU REMIND ME OF MY FATHER...
A QUICK STORY FOR YOU, NO MORE... I MUST HAVE BEEN SIX OR SEVEN. MY FATHER ACCUSED ME OF CUTTING EVERY ROSE IN THE GARDEN. TO PUNISH ME, HE TRIED TO TAKE AWAY MY ONLY DOLL.
AND?
I BURNED IT.
BUT YOU ARE NOT A CHILD ANYMORE. AND A MANOR IS NOT A DOLL...
AS YOU WISH, VIVIAN. IF YOU ARE SO EAGER TO KNOW WHAT YOU ARE MISSING...
BUT IF EVEN ONE WORD OF OUR CONVERSATION GETS OUT, REST ASSURED THAT WE SHALL BECOME THE FAVOURED QUARRY OF ALL THE SCUM OF THE UNDERWORLD, FROM PORTSMOUTH TO BRISTOL...
WHAT BYRON HAS DISCOVERED FAR OUTWEIGHS THE RICHES OF MOUNT POTOSI. MY BROTHER TURNED THE MYTH OF THE ELDORADO INTO REALITY.
HE SUCCEEDED, FOR THE GLORY OF ENGLAND...
HE FOUND THE CITY OF GUIANA-CAPAC!

11-

!! SO THAT'S IT! BUT MY POOR EDWARD, IT'S A FANTASY!

HE DREAMED OF NOTHING ELSE FOR YEARS! ALL THAT WAS NEEDED WAS SOME MALIGNANT FEVER, AND HE...

GUIANA-CAPAC EXISTS, MY LADY. MOXTECHICA HAS SEEN THE CITY. MY BROTHER'S CANE TOUCHED ITS PAVEMENT.

A LONG TIME AGO, DON ALMEDA WROTE: "THE INCA ATAHUALPA COULD HAVE PAID 100 TIMES HIS RANSOM TO PIZARRO IF HE HAD KNOWN ABOUT THE CITY'S EXISTENCE..." 100 TIMES A TEMPLE FILLED WITH GOLD...

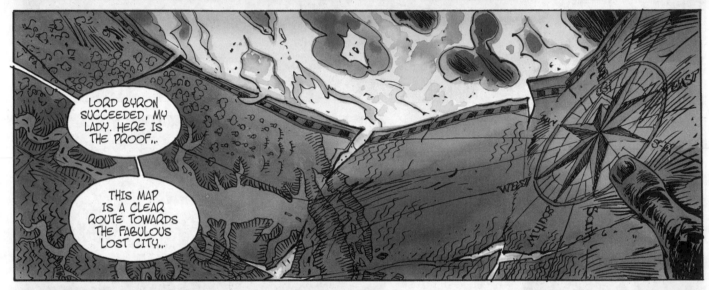

LORD BYRON SUCCEEDED, MY LADY. HERE IS THE PROOF...

THIS MAP IS A CLEAR ROUTE TOWARDS THE FABULOUS LOST CITY...

I WILL SAIL A SHIP TO THE COAST, THEN LEAD IT INTO THE MOUTH OF THE AMAZON RIVER.

FROM THERE, MOXTECHICA WILL LEAD US TO HIS VILLAGE BY THE JUNGLE WATERWAYS.

THIS MAP WILL BE OUR ARIADNE'S THREAD, AND BYRON WILL BE OUR GUIDE.

GOD ONLY KNOWS HOW THIS MAP SURVIVED THE CHURCH'S BOOK BURNINGS. WITHOUT IT, THE TRIP WOULD BE IMPOSSIBLE...

12-

WE MUST MOVE QUICKLY, IN ORDER TO ARRIVE JUST AFTER THE RAINY SEASON.

IT IS THE ONLY TIME WHEN THE WATER LEVEL THROUGHOUT THE DELTA IS HIGH ENOUGH TO LET OUR SHIP SAIL UP THROUGH THE JUNGLE.

AND WHAT SHALL BECOME OF ME?

DON'T WORRY, MY DEAR VIVIAN. WE HAVE NO INTENTION OF LEAVING YOU IN NEED,.. I THOUGHT OF A PLACE PERFECTLY SUITED TO YOUR PERSONALITY,..

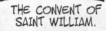

THE CONVENT OF SAINT WILLIAM.

EDWARD,..

WHY ARE YOU DOING THIS TO ME?

I DISLIKE PEOPLE OF YOUR ILK, VIVIAN. BUT WHETHER I LIKE IT OR NOT, YOU BEAR THE NAME OF HASTINGS. AN OLD AND GLORIOUS NAME. I WON'T LET YOU SULLY IT FURTHER.

SO, I'M BEING PUNISHED?

PROTECTED, MY LADY,..

,.. FROM YOURSELF,..

15

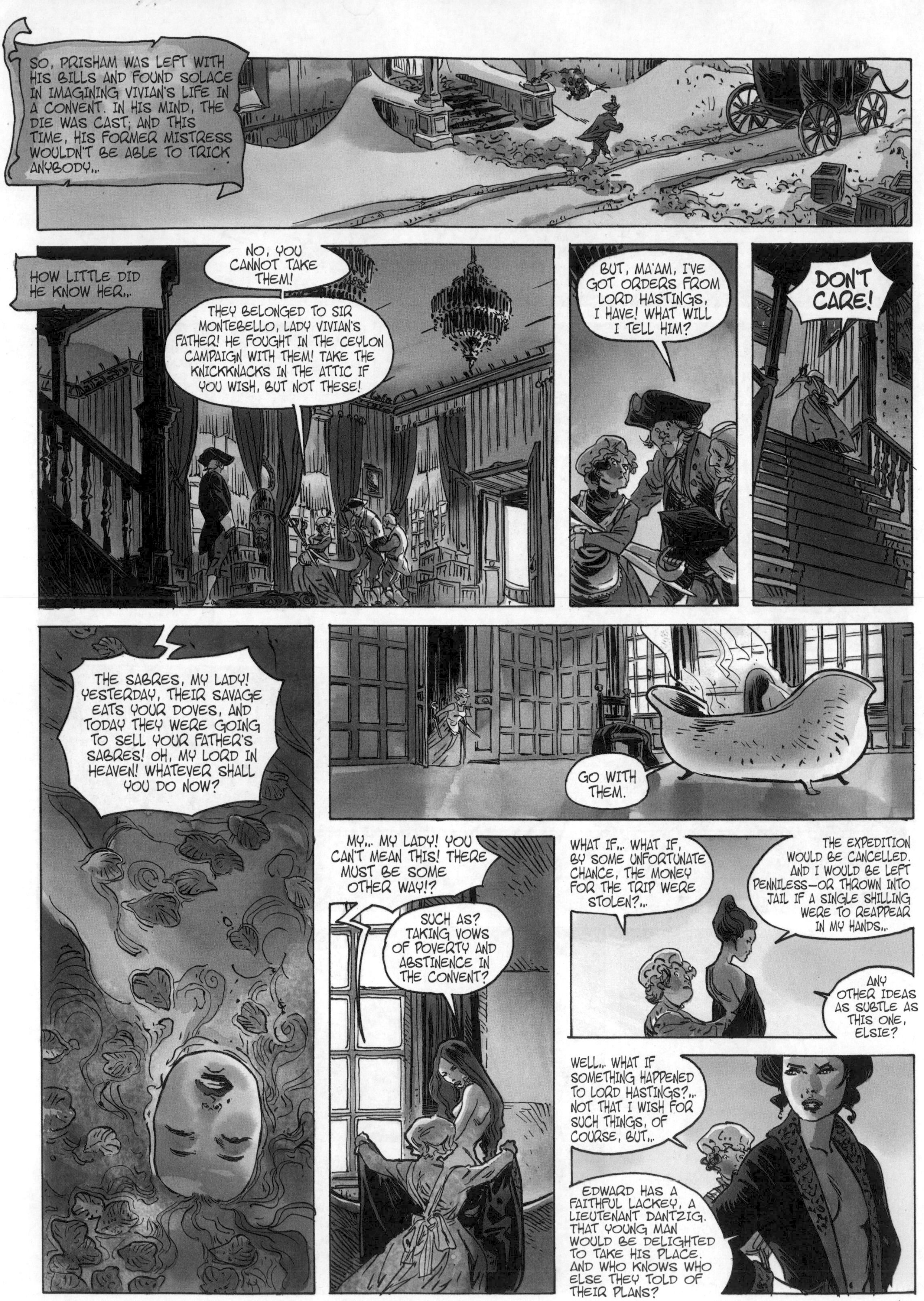

SO, PRISHAM WAS LEFT WITH HIS BILLS AND FOUND SOLACE IN IMAGINING VIVIAN'S LIFE IN A CONVENT. IN HIS MIND, THE DIE WAS CAST; AND THIS TIME, HIS FORMER MISTRESS WOULDN'T BE ABLE TO TRICK ANYBODY...
HOW LITTLE DID HE KNOW HER...
NO, YOU CANNOT TAKE THEM!
THEY BELONGED TO SIR MONTEBELLO, LADY VIVIAN'S FATHER! HE FOUGHT IN THE CEYLON CAMPAIGN WITH THEM! TAKE THE KNICKKNACKS IN THE ATTIC IF YOU WISH, BUT NOT THESE!
BUT, MA'AM, I'VE GOT ORDERS FROM LORD HASTINGS, I HAVE! WHAT WILL I TELL HIM?
DON'T CARE!
THE SABRES, MY LADY! YESTERDAY, THEIR SAVAGE EATS YOUR DOVES, AND TODAY THEY WERE GOING TO SELL YOUR FATHER'S SABRES! OH, MY LORD IN HEAVEN! WHATEVER SHALL YOU DO NOW?
GO WITH THEM.
MY... MY LADY! YOU CAN'T MEAN THIS! THERE MUST BE SOME OTHER WAY!?
SUCH AS? TAKING VOWS OF POVERTY AND ABSTINENCE IN THE CONVENT?
WHAT IF... WHAT IF, BY SOME UNFORTUNATE CHANCE, THE MONEY FOR THE TRIP WERE STOLEN?...
THE EXPEDITION WOULD BE CANCELLED. AND I WOULD BE LEFT PENNILESS—OR THROWN INTO JAIL IF A SINGLE SHILLING WERE TO REAPPEAR IN MY HANDS...
ANY OTHER IDEAS AS SUBTLE AS THIS ONE, ELSIE?
WELL... WHAT IF SOMETHING HAPPENED TO LORD HASTINGS?... NOT THAT I WISH FOR SUCH THINGS, OF COURSE, BUT...
EDWARD HAS A FAITHFUL LACKEY, A LIEUTENANT DANTZIG. THAT YOUNG MAN WOULD BE DELIGHTED TO TAKE HIS PLACE. AND WHO KNOWS WHO ELSE THEY TOLD OF THEIR PLANS?
14-

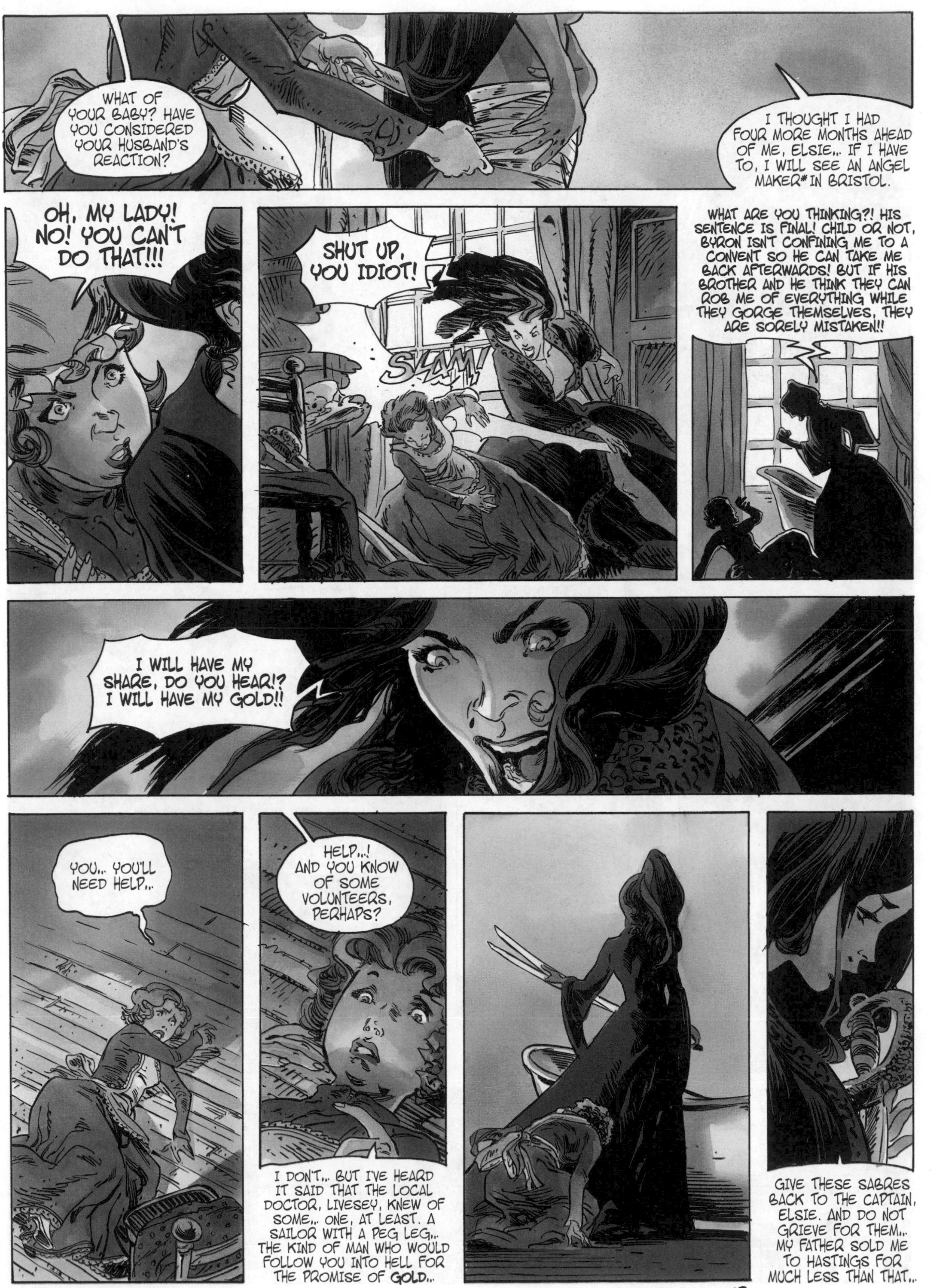
WHAT OF YOUR BABY? HAVE YOU CONSIDERED YOUR HUSBAND'S REACTION?
I THOUGHT I HAD FOUR MORE MONTHS AHEAD OF ME, ELSIE,.. IF I HAVE TO, I WILL SEE AN ANGEL MAKER* IN BRISTOL.
OH, MY LADY! NO! YOU CAN'T DO THAT!!!
SHUT UP, YOU IDIOT!
SLAM!
WHAT ARE YOU THINKING?! HIS SENTENCE IS FINAL! CHILD OR NOT, BYRON ISN'T CONFINING ME TO A CONVENT SO HE CAN TAKE ME BACK AFTERWARDS! BUT IF HIS BROTHER AND HE THINK THEY CAN ROB ME OF EVERYTHING WHILE THEY GORGE THEMSELVES, THEY ARE SORELY MISTAKEN!!
I WILL HAVE MY SHARE, DO YOU HEAR!? I WILL HAVE MY GOLD!!
YOU,.. YOU'LL NEED HELP,..
HELP,..! AND YOU KNOW OF SOME VOLUNTEERS, PERHAPS?
I DON'T,.. BUT I'VE HEARD IT SAID THAT THE LOCAL DOCTOR, LIVESEY, KNEW OF SOME,.. ONE, AT LEAST. A SAILOR WITH A PEG LEG,.. THE KIND OF MAN WHO WOULD FOLLOW YOU INTO HELL FOR THE PROMISE OF GOLD,..
GIVE THESE SABRES BACK TO THE CAPTAIN, ELSIE. AND DO NOT GRIEVE FOR THEM,.. MY FATHER SOLD ME TO HASTINGS FOR MUCH LESS THAN THAT,..
15-

*A NICKNAME FOR A BACK ALLEY ABORTIONIST

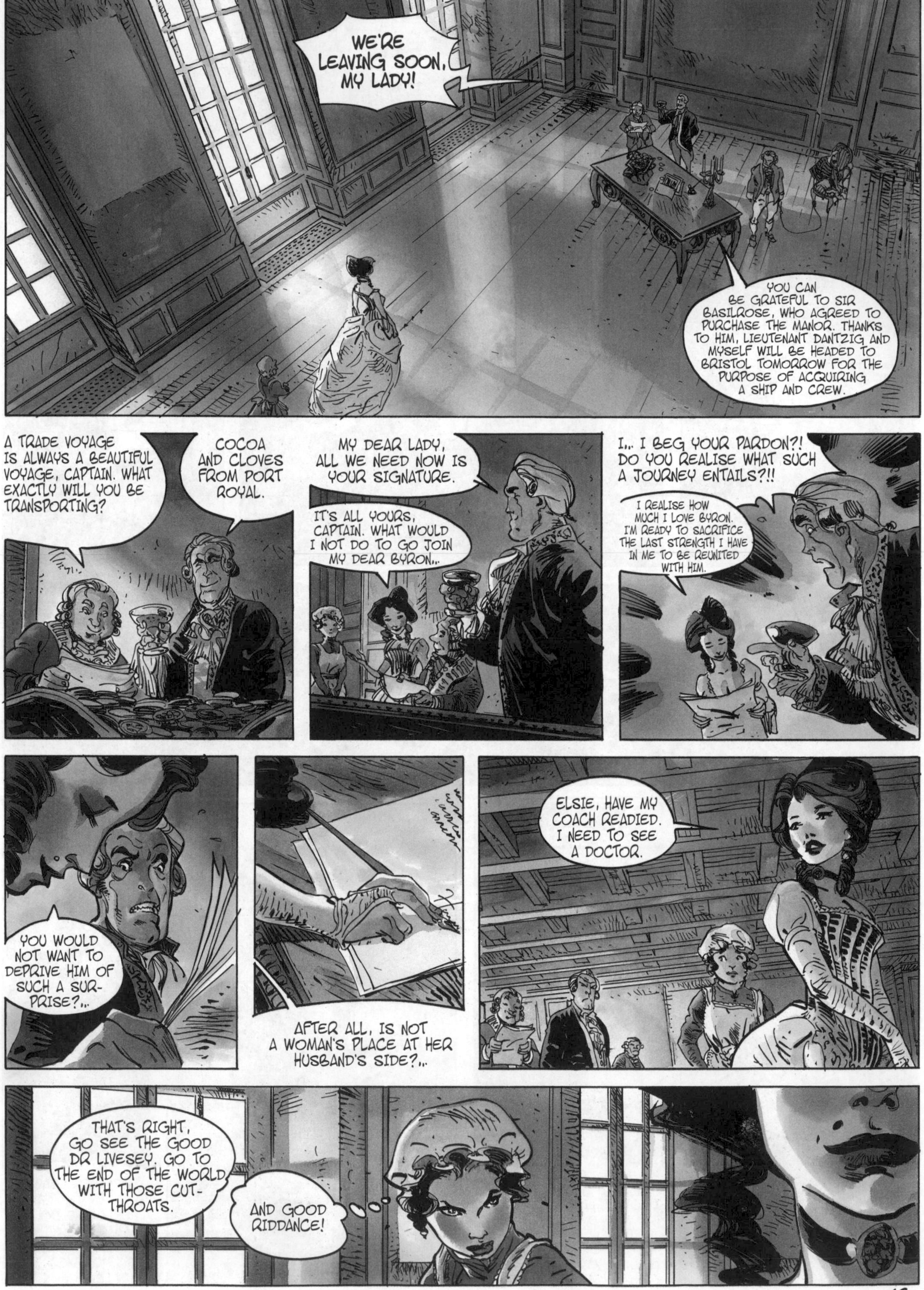
WE'RE LEAVING SOON, MY LADY!
YOU CAN BE GRATEFUL TO SIR BASILROSE, WHO AGREED TO PURCHASE THE MANOR. THANKS TO HIM, LIEUTENANT DANTZIG AND MYSELF WILL BE HEADED TO BRISTOL TOMORROW FOR THE PURPOSE OF ACQUIRING A SHIP AND CREW.
A TRADE VOYAGE IS ALWAYS A BEAUTIFUL VOYAGE, CAPTAIN. WHAT EXACTLY WILL YOU BE TRANSPORTING?
COCOA AND CLOVES FROM PORT ROYAL.
MY DEAR LADY, ALL WE NEED NOW IS YOUR SIGNATURE.
IT'S ALL YOURS, CAPTAIN. WHAT WOULD I NOT DO TO GO JOIN MY DEAR BYRON...
I... I BEG YOUR PARDON?! DO YOU REALISE WHAT SUCH A JOURNEY ENTAILS?!!
I REALISE HOW MUCH I LOVE BYRON. I'M READY TO SACRIFICE THE LAST STRENGTH I HAVE IN ME TO BE REUNITED WITH HIM.
YOU WOULD NOT WANT TO DEPRIVE HIM OF SUCH A SURPRISE?...
AFTER ALL, IS NOT A WOMAN'S PLACE AT HER HUSBAND'S SIDE?...
ELSIE, HAVE MY COACH READIED. I NEED TO SEE A DOCTOR.
THAT'S RIGHT, GO SEE THE GOOD DR LIVESEY. GO TO THE END OF THE WORLD WITH THOSE CUT-THROATS.
AND GOOD RIDDANCE!
16-

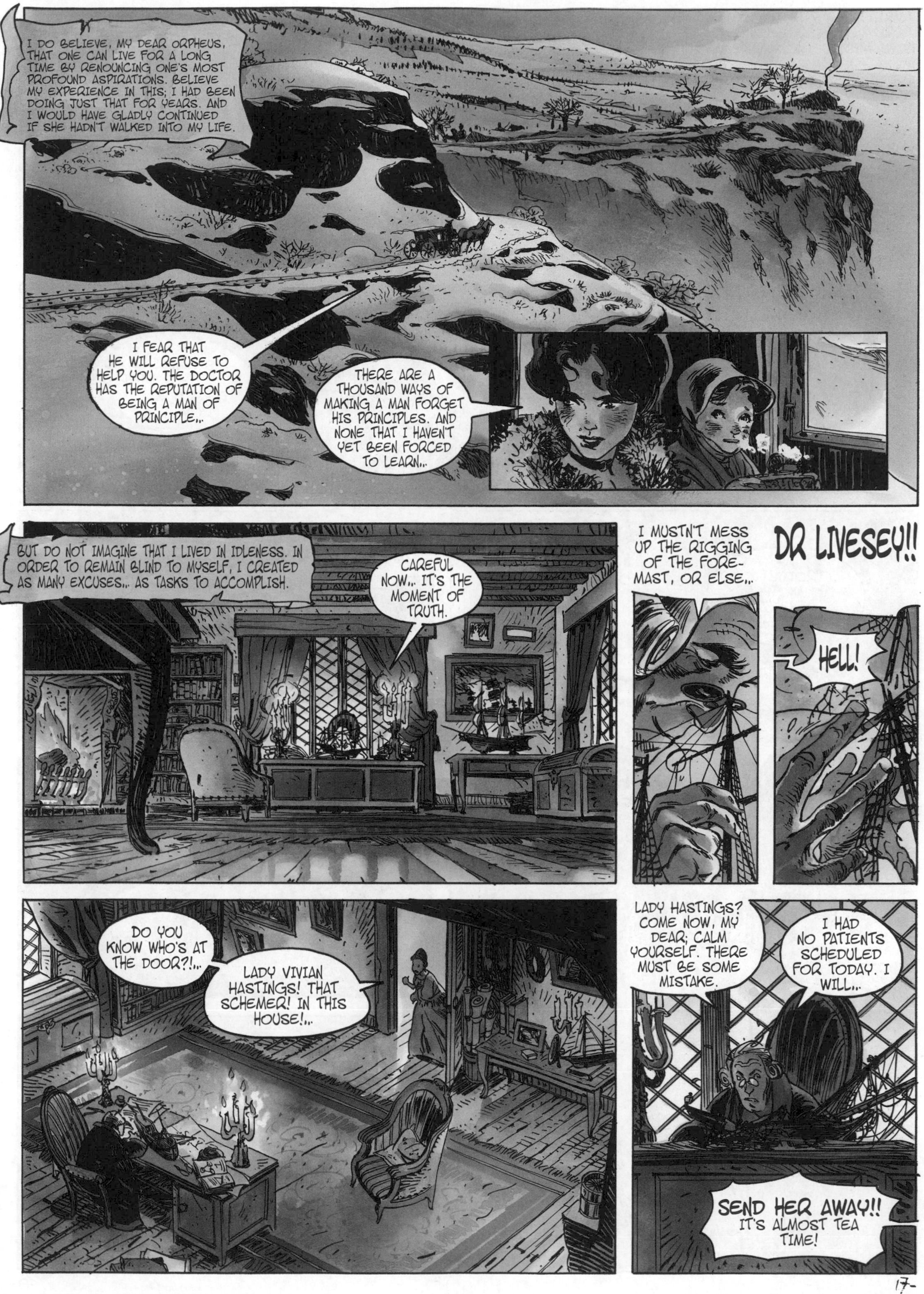
I DO BELIEVE, MY DEAR ORPHEUS, THAT ONE CAN LIVE FOR A LONG TIME BY RENOUNCING ONE'S MOST PROFOUND ASPIRATIONS. BELIEVE MY EXPERIENCE IN THIS; I HAD BEEN DOING JUST THAT FOR YEARS. AND I WOULD HAVE GLADLY CONTINUED IF SHE HADN'T WALKED INTO MY LIFE.
I FEAR THAT HE WILL REFUSE TO HELP YOU. THE DOCTOR HAS THE REPUTATION OF BEING A MAN OF PRINCIPLE...
THERE ARE A THOUSAND WAYS OF MAKING A MAN FORGET HIS PRINCIPLES. AND NONE THAT I HAVEN'T YET BEEN FORCED TO LEARN...
BUT DO NOT IMAGINE THAT I LIVED IN IDLENESS. IN ORDER TO REMAIN BLIND TO MYSELF, I CREATED AS MANY EXCUSES... AS TASKS TO ACCOMPLISH.
CAREFUL NOW... IT'S THE MOMENT OF TRUTH.
I MUSTN'T MESS UP THE RIGGING OF THE FORE-MAST, OR ELSE...
DR LIVESEY!!
HELL!
DO YOU KNOW WHO'S AT THE DOOR?!...
LADY VIVIAN HASTINGS! THAT SCHEMER! IN THIS HOUSE!...
LADY HASTINGS? COME NOW, MY DEAR; CALM YOURSELF. THERE MUST BE SOME MISTAKE.
I HAD NO PATIENTS SCHEDULED FOR TODAY. I WILL...
SEND HER AWAY!! IT'S ALMOST TEA TIME!
17-

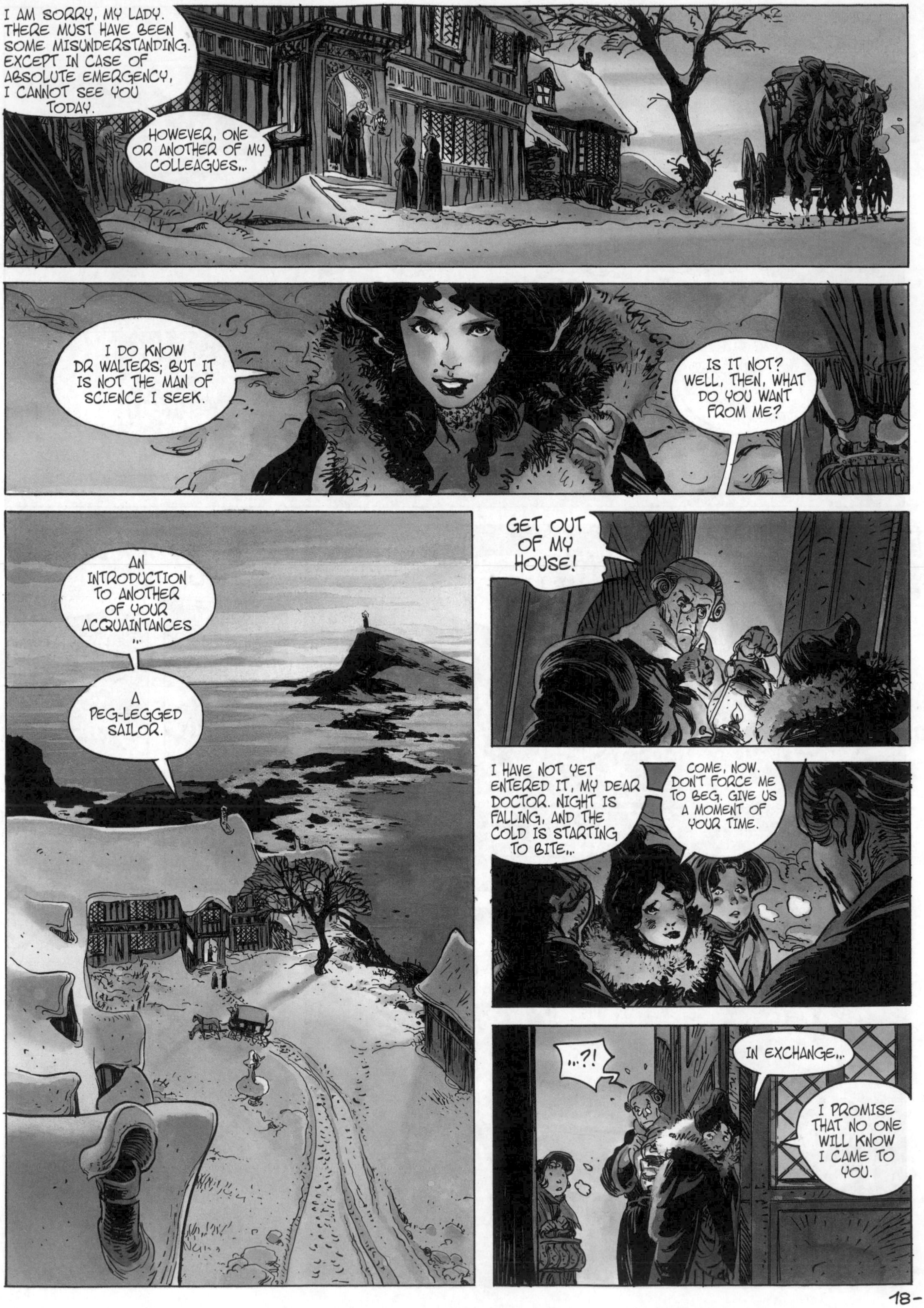
I AM SORRY, MY LADY. THERE MUST HAVE BEEN SOME MISUNDERSTANDING. EXCEPT IN CASE OF ABSOLUTE EMERGENCY, I CANNOT SEE YOU TODAY.
HOWEVER, ONE OR ANOTHER OF MY COLLEAGUES...
I DO KNOW DR WALTERS; BUT IT IS NOT THE MAN OF SCIENCE I SEEK.
IS IT NOT? WELL, THEN, WHAT DO YOU WANT FROM ME?
AN INTRODUCTION TO ANOTHER OF YOUR ACQUAINTANCES ...
A PEG-LEGGED SAILOR.
GET OUT OF MY HOUSE!
I HAVE NOT YET ENTERED IT, MY DEAR DOCTOR. NIGHT IS FALLING, AND THE COLD IS STARTING TO BITE...
COME, NOW. DON'T FORCE ME TO BEG. GIVE US A MOMENT OF YOUR TIME.
...?!
IN EXCHANGE...
I PROMISE THAT NO ONE WILL KNOW I CAME TO YOU.
18-

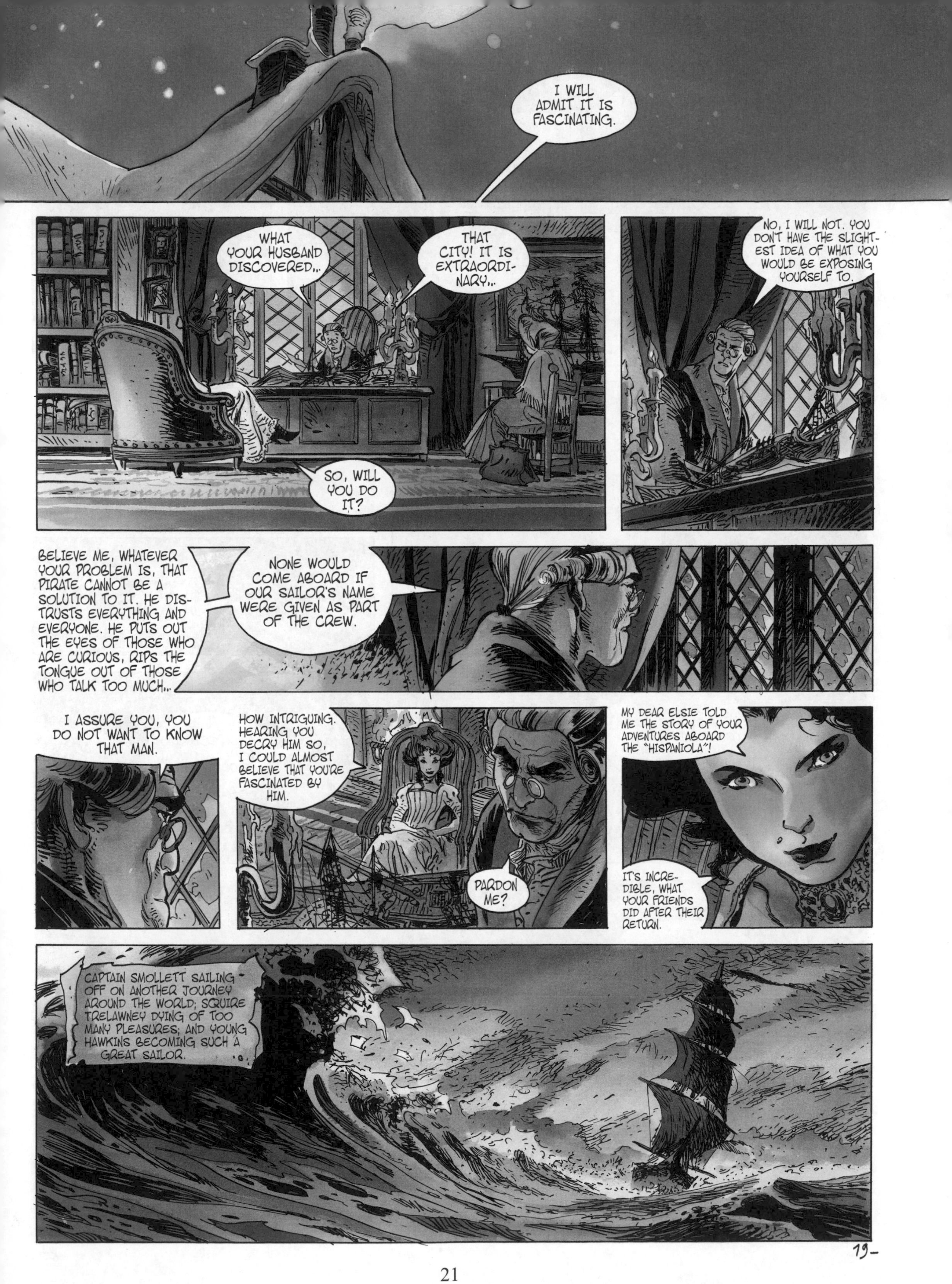

I WILL ADMIT IT IS FASCINATING.
WHAT YOUR HUSBAND DISCOVERED...
THAT CITY! IT IS EXTRAORDINARY...
SO, WILL YOU DO IT?
NO, I WILL NOT. YOU DON'T HAVE THE SLIGHTEST IDEA OF WHAT YOU WOULD BE EXPOSING YOURSELF TO.
BELIEVE ME, WHATEVER YOUR PROBLEM IS, THAT PIRATE CANNOT BE A SOLUTION TO IT. HE DISTRUSTS EVERYTHING AND EVERYONE. HE PUTS OUT THE EYES OF THOSE WHO ARE CURIOUS, RIPS THE TONGUE OUT OF THOSE WHO TALK TOO MUCH...
NONE WOULD COME ABOARD IF OUR SAILOR'S NAME WERE GIVEN AS PART OF THE CREW.
I ASSURE YOU, YOU DO NOT WANT TO KNOW THAT MAN.
HOW INTRIGUING. HEARING YOU DECRY HIM SO, I COULD ALMOST BELIEVE THAT YOU'RE FASCINATED BY HIM.
PARDON ME?
MY DEAR ELSIE TOLD ME THE STORY OF YOUR ADVENTURES ABOARD THE "HISPANIOLA"!
IT'S INCREDIBLE, WHAT YOUR FRIENDS DID AFTER THEIR RETURN.
CAPTAIN SMOLLETT SAILING OFF ON ANOTHER JOURNEY AROUND THE WORLD; SQUIRE TRELAWNEY DYING OF TOO MANY PLEASURES; AND YOUNG HAWKINS BECOMING SUCH A GREAT SAILOR.
19

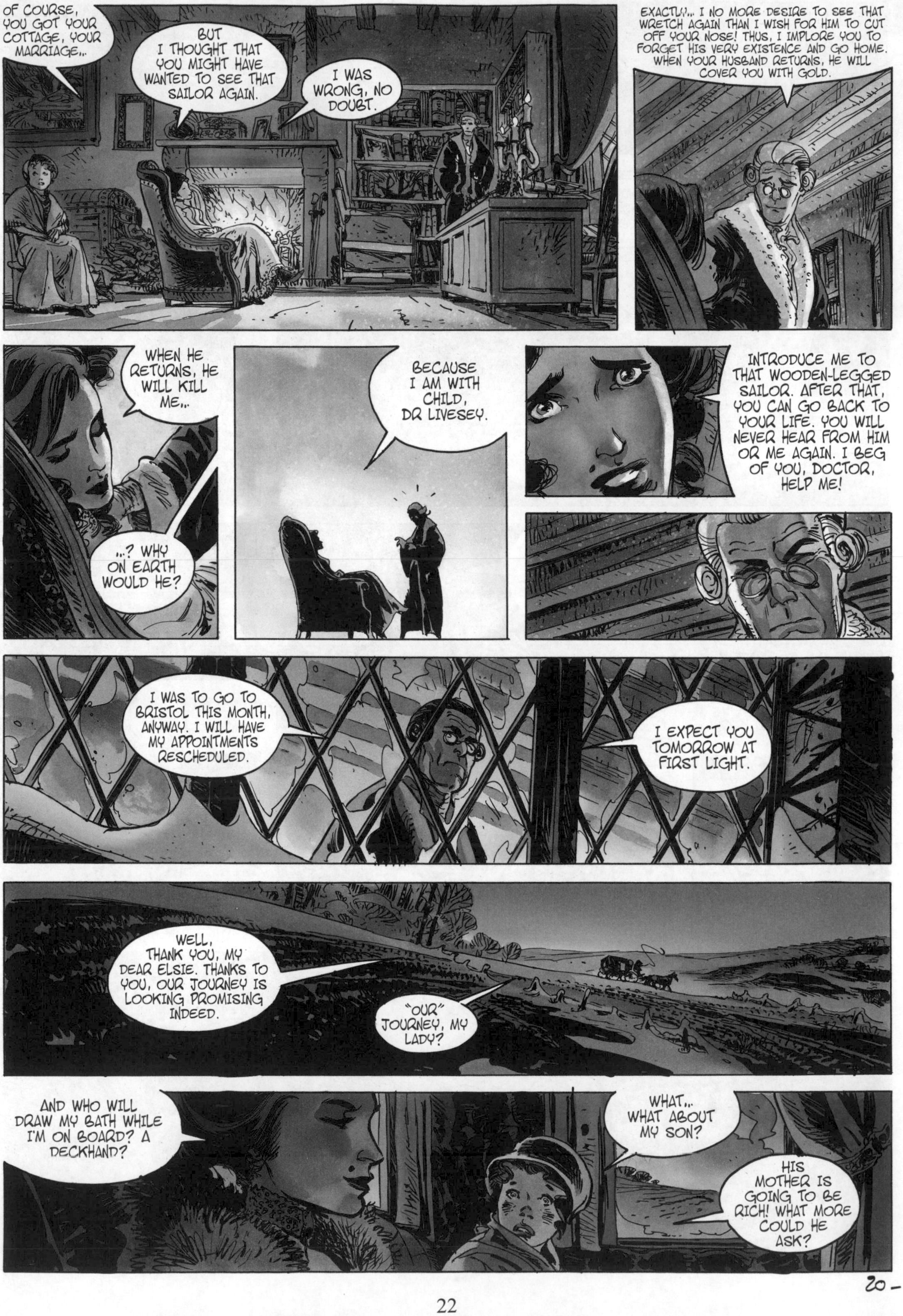

OF COURSE, YOU GOT YOUR COTTAGE, YOUR MARRIAGE...
BUT I THOUGHT THAT YOU MIGHT HAVE WANTED TO SEE THAT SAILOR AGAIN.
I WAS WRONG, NO DOUBT.
EXACTLY... I NO MORE DESIRE TO SEE THAT WRETCH AGAIN THAN I WISH FOR HIM TO CUT OFF YOUR NOSE! THUS, I IMPLORE YOU TO FORGET HIS VERY EXISTENCE AND GO HOME. WHEN YOUR HUSBAND RETURNS, HE WILL COVER YOU WITH GOLD.
WHEN HE RETURNS, HE WILL KILL ME...
...? WHY ON EARTH WOULD HE?
BECAUSE I AM WITH CHILD, DR LIVESEY.
INTRODUCE ME TO THAT WOODEN-LEGGED SAILOR. AFTER THAT, YOU CAN GO BACK TO YOUR LIFE. YOU WILL NEVER HEAR FROM HIM OR ME AGAIN. I BEG OF YOU, DOCTOR, HELP ME!
I WAS TO GO TO BRISTOL THIS MONTH, ANYWAY. I WILL HAVE MY APPOINTMENTS RESCHEDULED.
I EXPECT YOU TOMORROW AT FIRST LIGHT.
WELL, THANK YOU, MY DEAR ELSIE. THANKS TO YOU, OUR JOURNEY IS LOOKING PROMISING INDEED.
"OUR" JOURNEY, MY LADY?
AND WHO WILL DRAW MY BATH WHILE I'M ON BOARD? A DECKHAND?
WHAT... WHAT ABOUT MY SON?
HIS MOTHER IS GOING TO BE RICH! WHAT MORE COULD HE ASK?


20 -

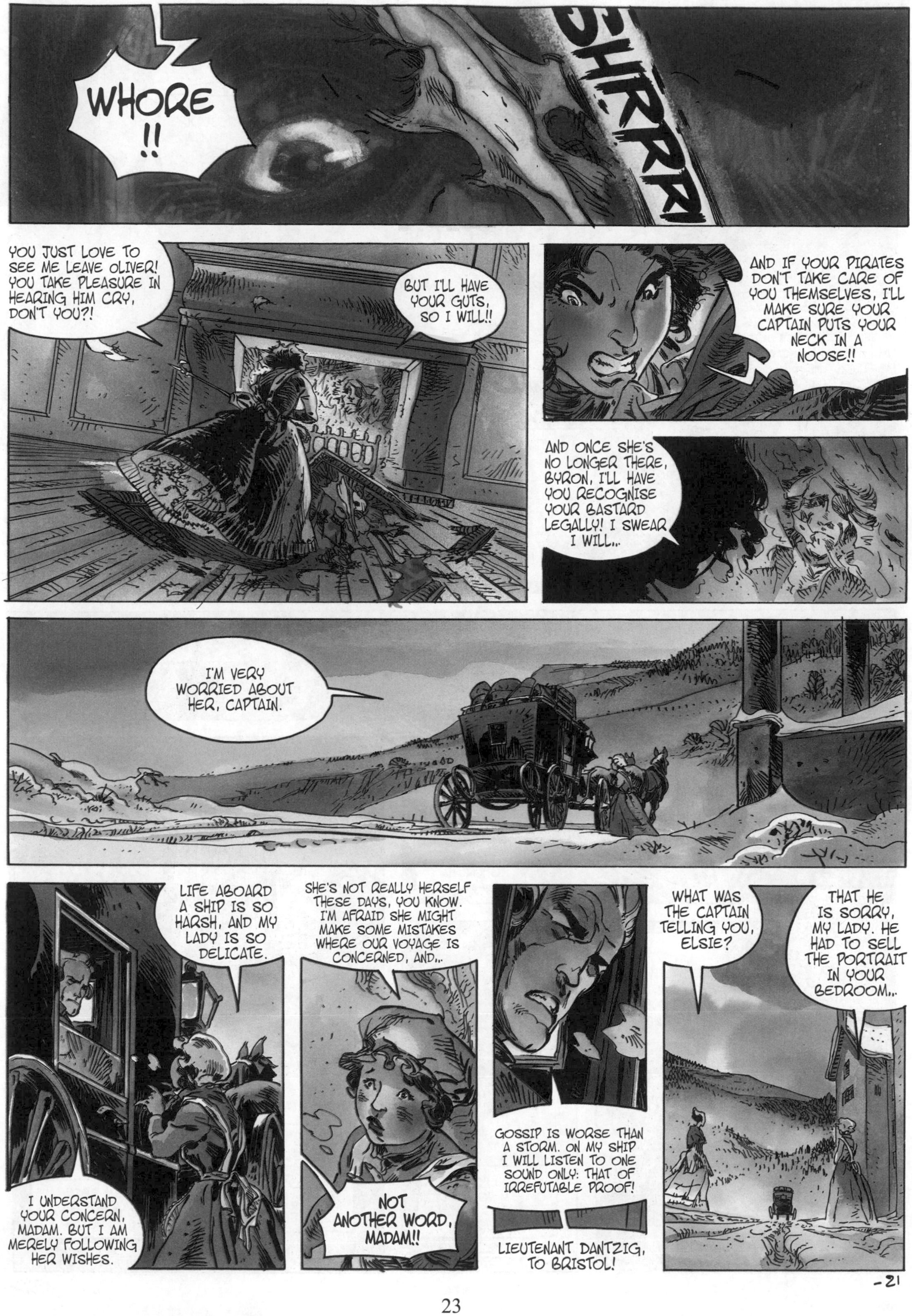
WHORE !!
SHRRR
YOU JUST LOVE TO SEE ME LEAVE OLIVER! YOU TAKE PLEASURE IN HEARING HIM CRY, DON'T YOU?!
BUT I'LL HAVE YOUR GUTS, SO I WILL!!
AND IF YOUR PIRATES DON'T TAKE CARE OF YOU THEMSELVES, I'LL MAKE SURE YOUR CAPTAIN PUTS YOUR NECK IN A NOOSE!!
AND ONCE SHE'S NO LONGER THERE, BYRON, I'LL HAVE YOU RECOGNISE YOUR BASTARD LEGALLY! I SWEAR I WILL..
I'M VERY WORRIED ABOUT HER, CAPTAIN.
LIFE ABOARD A SHIP IS SO HARSH, AND MY LADY IS SO DELICATE.
I UNDERSTAND YOUR CONCERN, MADAM. BUT I AM MERELY FOLLOWING HER WISHES.
SHE'S NOT REALLY HERSELF THESE DAYS, YOU KNOW. I'M AFRAID SHE MIGHT MAKE SOME MISTAKES WHERE OUR VOYAGE IS CONCERNED, AND..
NOT ANOTHER WORD, MADAM!!
GOSSIP IS WORSE THAN A STORM. ON MY SHIP I WILL LISTEN TO ONE SOUND ONLY: THAT OF IRREFUTABLE PROOF!
LIEUTENANT DANTZIG, TO BRISTOL!
WHAT WAS THE CAPTAIN TELLING YOU, ELSIE?
THAT HE IS SORRY, MY LADY. HE HAD TO SELL THE PORTRAIT IN YOUR BEDROOM..
-21

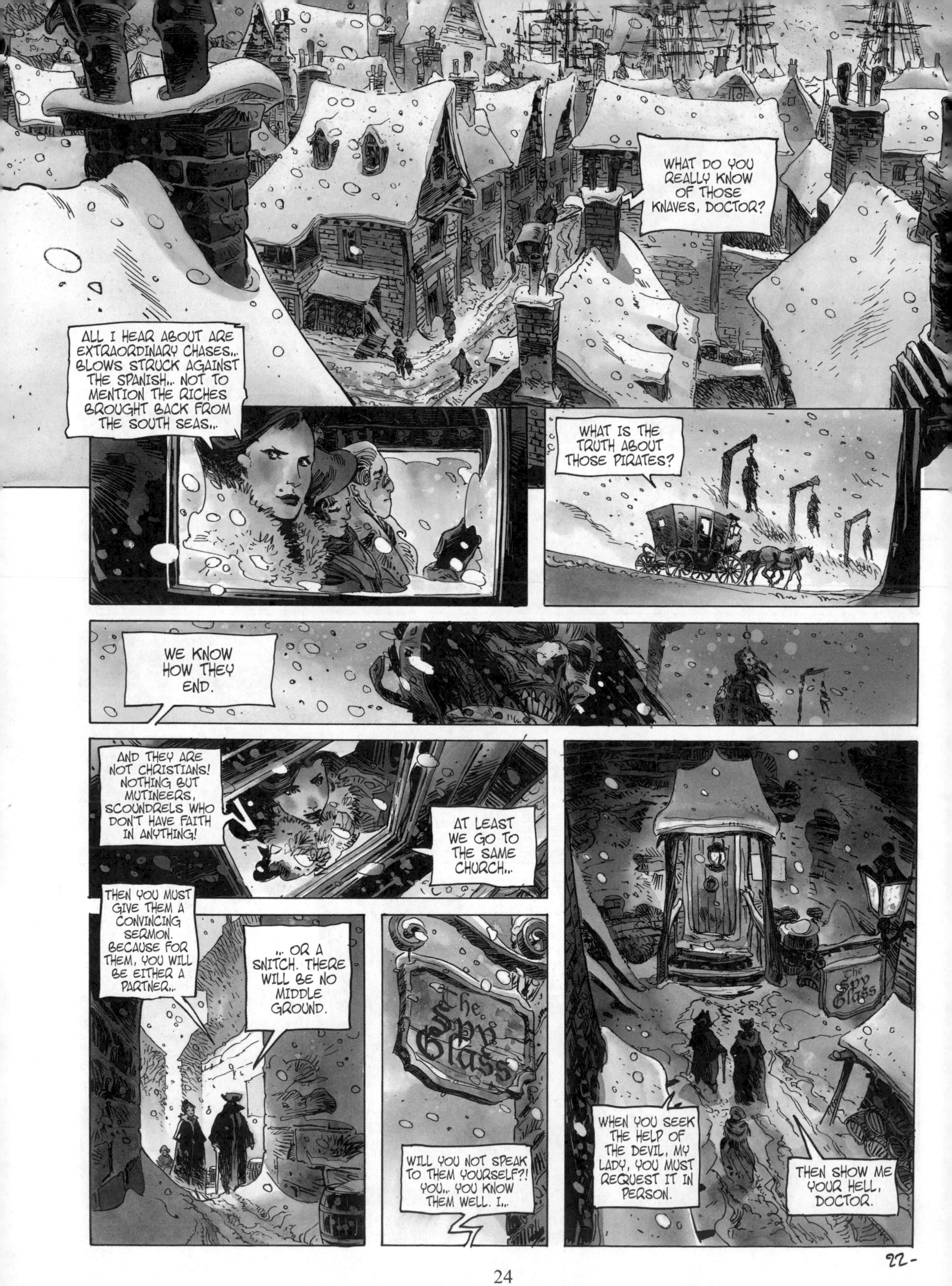
WHAT DO YOU REALLY KNOW OF THOSE KNAVES, DOCTOR?
ALL I HEAR ABOUT ARE EXTRAORDINARY CHASES... BLOWS STRUCK AGAINST THE SPANISH... NOT TO MENTION THE RICHES BROUGHT BACK FROM THE SOUTH SEAS...
WHAT IS THE TRUTH ABOUT THOSE PIRATES?
WE KNOW HOW THEY END.
AND THEY ARE NOT CHRISTIANS! NOTHING BUT MUTINEERS, SCOUNDRELS WHO DON'T HAVE FAITH IN ANYTHING!
AT LEAST WE GO TO THE SAME CHURCH...
THEN YOU MUST GIVE THEM A CONVINCING SERMON. BECAUSE FOR THEM, YOU WILL BE EITHER A PARTNER...
... OR A SNITCH. THERE WILL BE NO MIDDLE GROUND.
The Spy Glass
WILL YOU NOT SPEAK TO THEM YOURSELF?! YOU... YOU KNOW THEM WELL. I...
The Spy Glass
WHEN YOU SEEK THE HELP OF THE DEVIL, MY LADY, YOU MUST REQUEST IT IN PERSON.
THEN SHOW ME YOUR HELL, DOCTOR.
22-

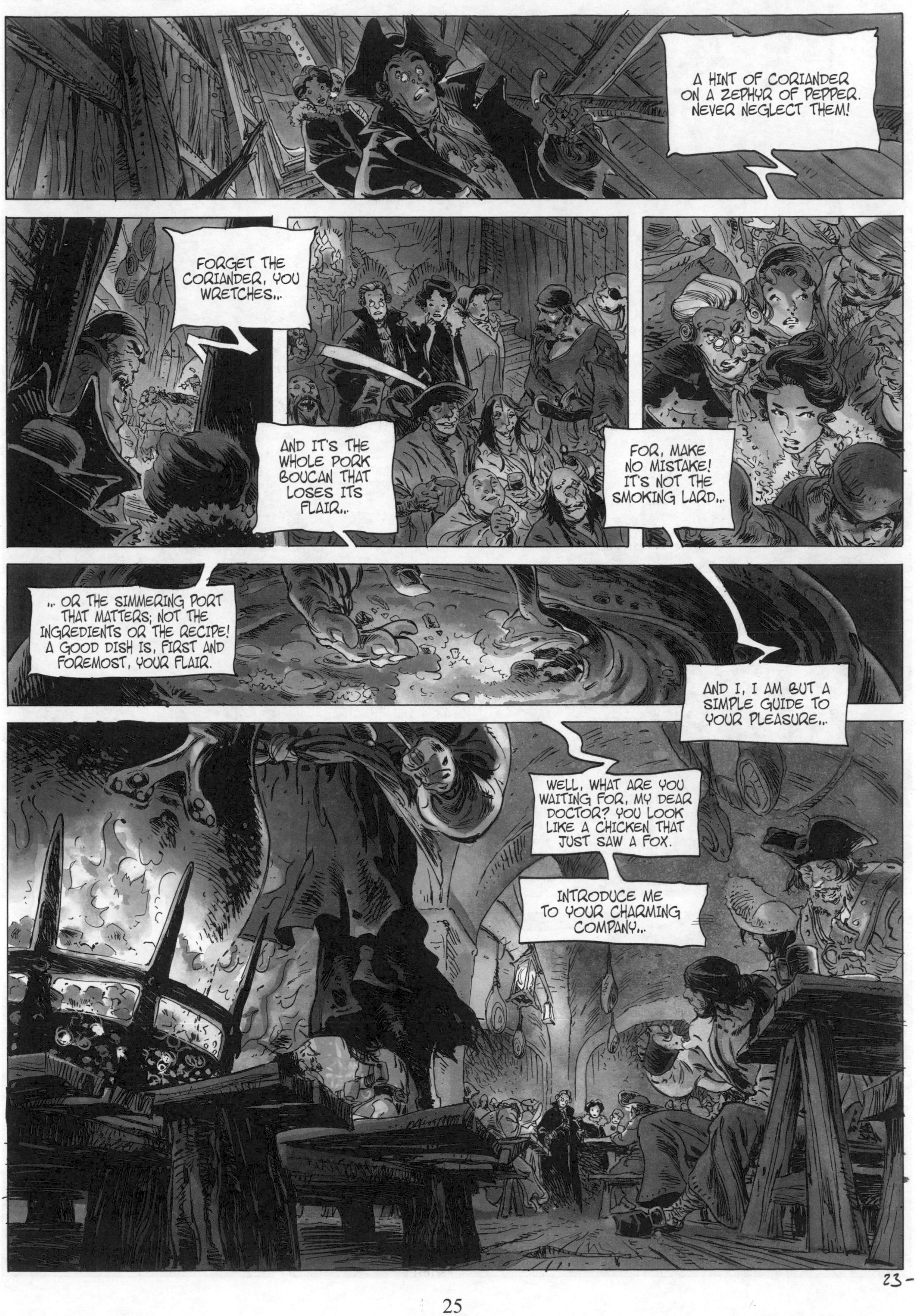
A HINT OF CORIANDER ON A ZEPHYR OF PEPPER. NEVER NEGLECT THEM!
FORGET THE CORIANDER, YOU WRETCHES...
AND IT'S THE WHOLE PORK BOUCAN THAT LOSES ITS FLAIR...
FOR, MAKE NO MISTAKE! IT'S NOT THE SMOKING LARD...
... OR THE SIMMERING PORT THAT MATTERS; NOT THE INGREDIENTS OR THE RECIPE! A GOOD DISH IS, FIRST AND FOREMOST, YOUR FLAIR.
AND I, I AM BUT A SIMPLE GUIDE TO YOUR PLEASURE...
WELL, WHAT ARE YOU WAITING FOR, MY DEAR DOCTOR? YOU LOOK LIKE A CHICKEN THAT JUST SAW A FOX.
INTRODUCE ME TO YOUR CHARMING COMPANY...
23-

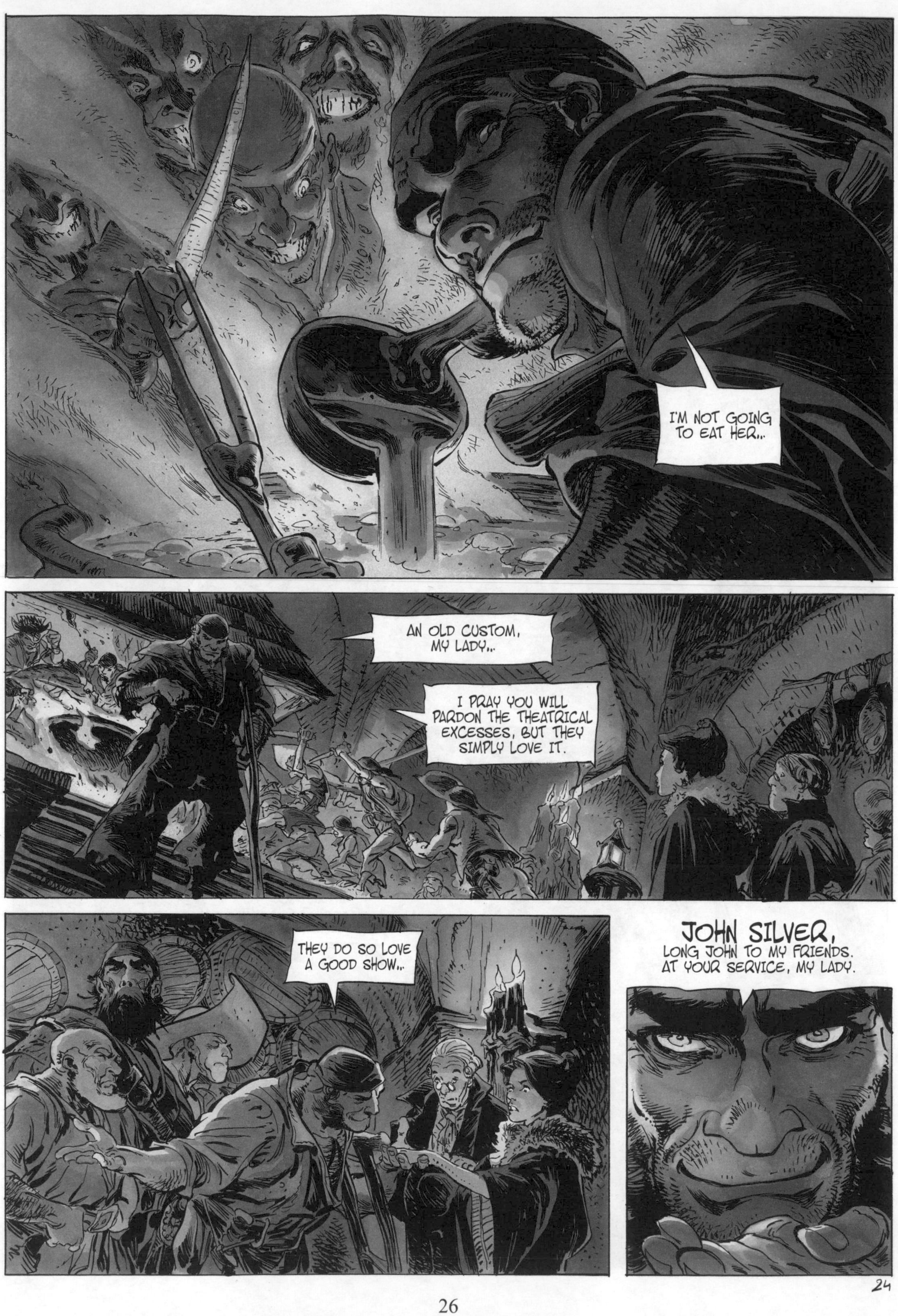
I'M NOT GOING TO EAT HER...
AN OLD CUSTOM, MY LADY...
I PRAY YOU WILL PARDON THE THEATRICAL EXCESSES, BUT THEY SIMPLY LOVE IT.
THEY DO SO LOVE A GOOD SHOW...
JOHN SILVER,
LONG JOHN TO MY FRIENDS. AT YOUR SERVICE, MY LADY.
24

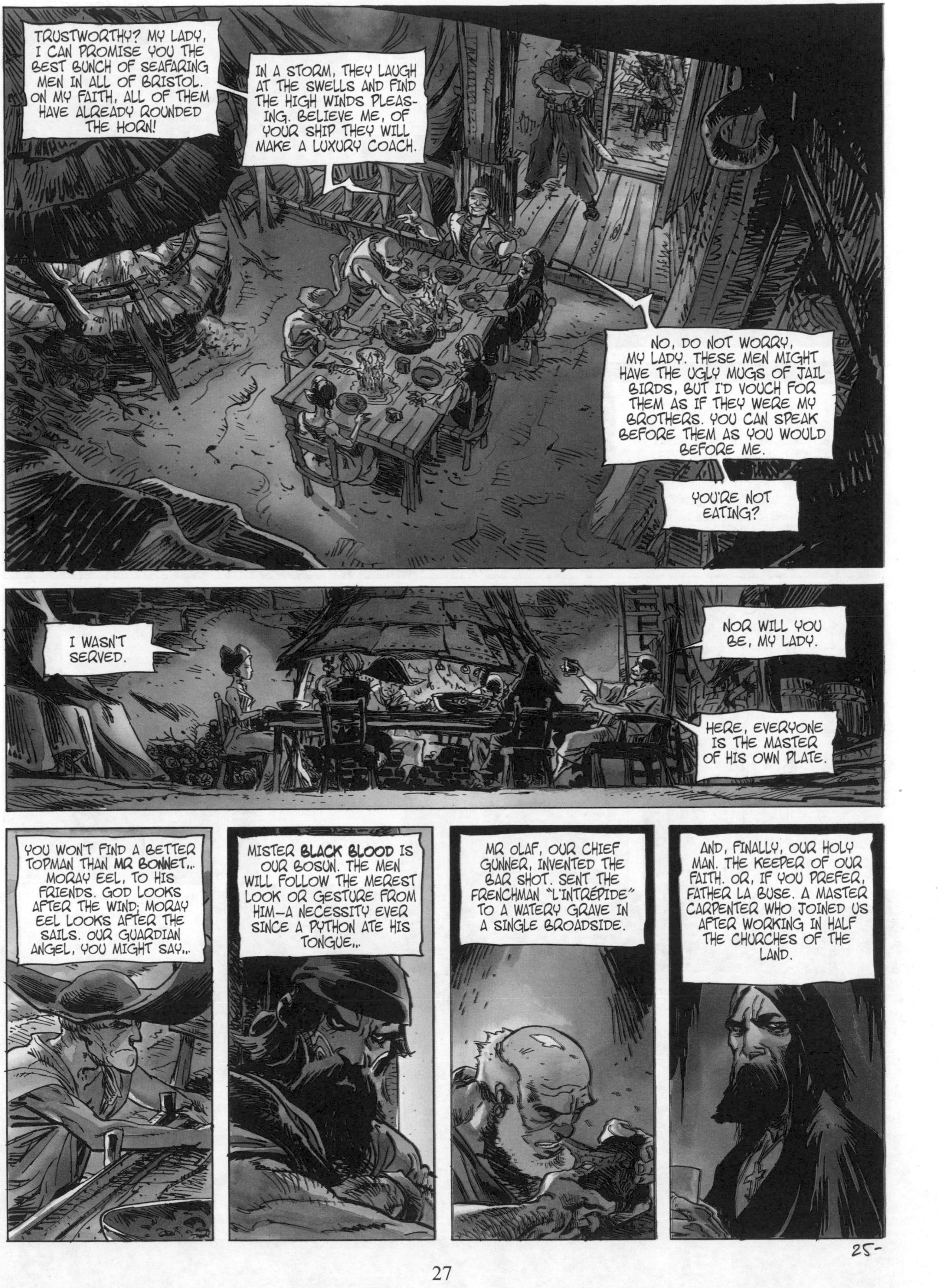
TRUSTWORTHY? MY LADY, I CAN PROMISE YOU THE BEST BUNCH OF SEAFARING MEN IN ALL OF BRISTOL. ON MY FAITH, ALL OF THEM HAVE ALREADY ROUNDED THE HORN!
IN A STORM, THEY LAUGH AT THE SWELLS AND FIND THE HIGH WINDS PLEASING. BELIEVE ME, OF YOUR SHIP THEY WILL MAKE A LUXURY COACH.
NO, DO NOT WORRY, MY LADY. THESE MEN MIGHT HAVE THE UGLY MUGS OF JAIL BIRDS, BUT I'D VOUCH FOR THEM AS IF THEY WERE MY BROTHERS. YOU CAN SPEAK BEFORE THEM AS YOU WOULD BEFORE ME.
YOU'RE NOT EATING?
I WASN'T SERVED.
NOR WILL YOU BE, MY LADY.
HERE, EVERYONE IS THE MASTER OF HIS OWN PLATE.
YOU WON'T FIND A BETTER TOPMAN THAN MR BONNET... MORAY EEL, TO HIS FRIENDS. GOD LOOKS AFTER THE WIND; MORAY EEL LOOKS AFTER THE SAILS. OUR GUARDIAN ANGEL, YOU MIGHT SAY...
MISTER BLACK BLOOD IS OUR BOSUN. THE MEN WILL FOLLOW THE MEREST LOOK OR GESTURE FROM HIM—A NECESSITY EVER SINCE A PYTHON ATE HIS TONGUE...
MR OLAF, OUR CHIEF GUNNER, INVENTED THE BAR SHOT. SENT THE FRENCHMAN "L'INTRÉPIDE" TO A WATERY GRAVE IN A SINGLE BROADSIDE.
AND, FINALLY, OUR HOLY MAN. THE KEEPER OF OUR FAITH. OR, IF YOU PREFER, FATHER LA BUSE. A MASTER CARPENTER WHO JOINED US AFTER WORKING IN HALF THE CHURCHES OF THE LAND.
25-

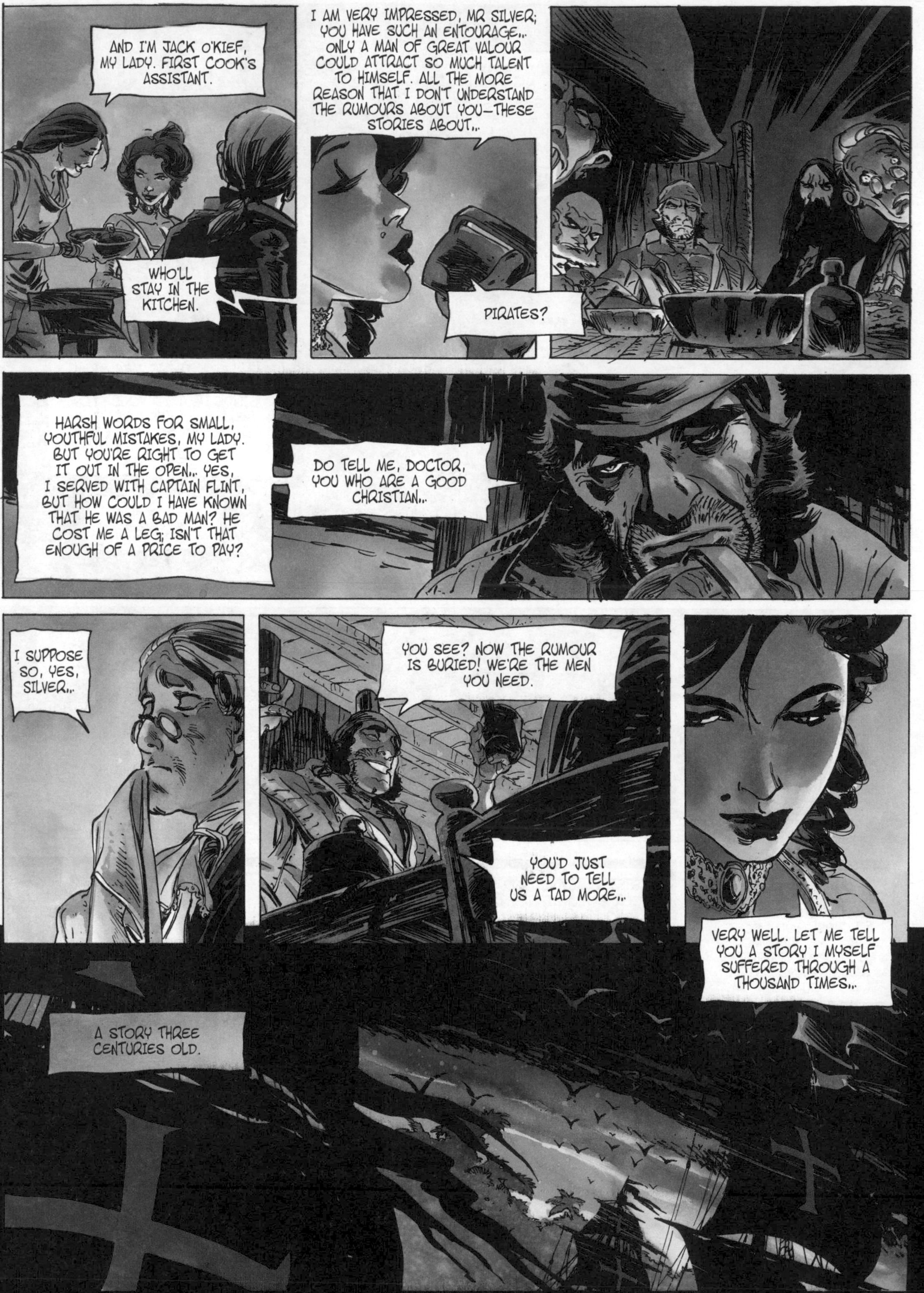
AND I'M JACK O'KIEF, MY LADY. FIRST COOK'S ASSISTANT.
WHO'LL STAY IN THE KITCHEN.
I AM VERY IMPRESSED, MR SILVER; YOU HAVE SUCH AN ENTOURAGE... ONLY A MAN OF GREAT VALOUR COULD ATTRACT SO MUCH TALENT TO HIMSELF. ALL THE MORE REASON THAT I DON'T UNDERSTAND THE RUMOURS ABOUT YOU—THESE STORIES ABOUT...
PIRATES?
HARSH WORDS FOR SMALL, YOUTHFUL MISTAKES, MY LADY. BUT YOU'RE RIGHT TO GET IT OUT IN THE OPEN... YES, I SERVED WITH CAPTAIN FLINT, BUT HOW COULD I HAVE KNOWN THAT HE WAS A BAD MAN? HE COST ME A LEG; ISN'T THAT ENOUGH OF A PRICE TO PAY?
DO TELL ME, DOCTOR, YOU WHO ARE A GOOD CHRISTIAN...
I SUPPOSE SO, YES, SILVER...
YOU SEE? NOW THE RUMOUR IS BURIED! WE'RE THE MEN YOU NEED.
YOU'D JUST NEED TO TELL US A TAD MORE...
VERY WELL. LET ME TELL YOU A STORY I MYSELF SUFFERED THROUGH A THOUSAND TIMES...
A STORY THREE CENTURIES OLD.

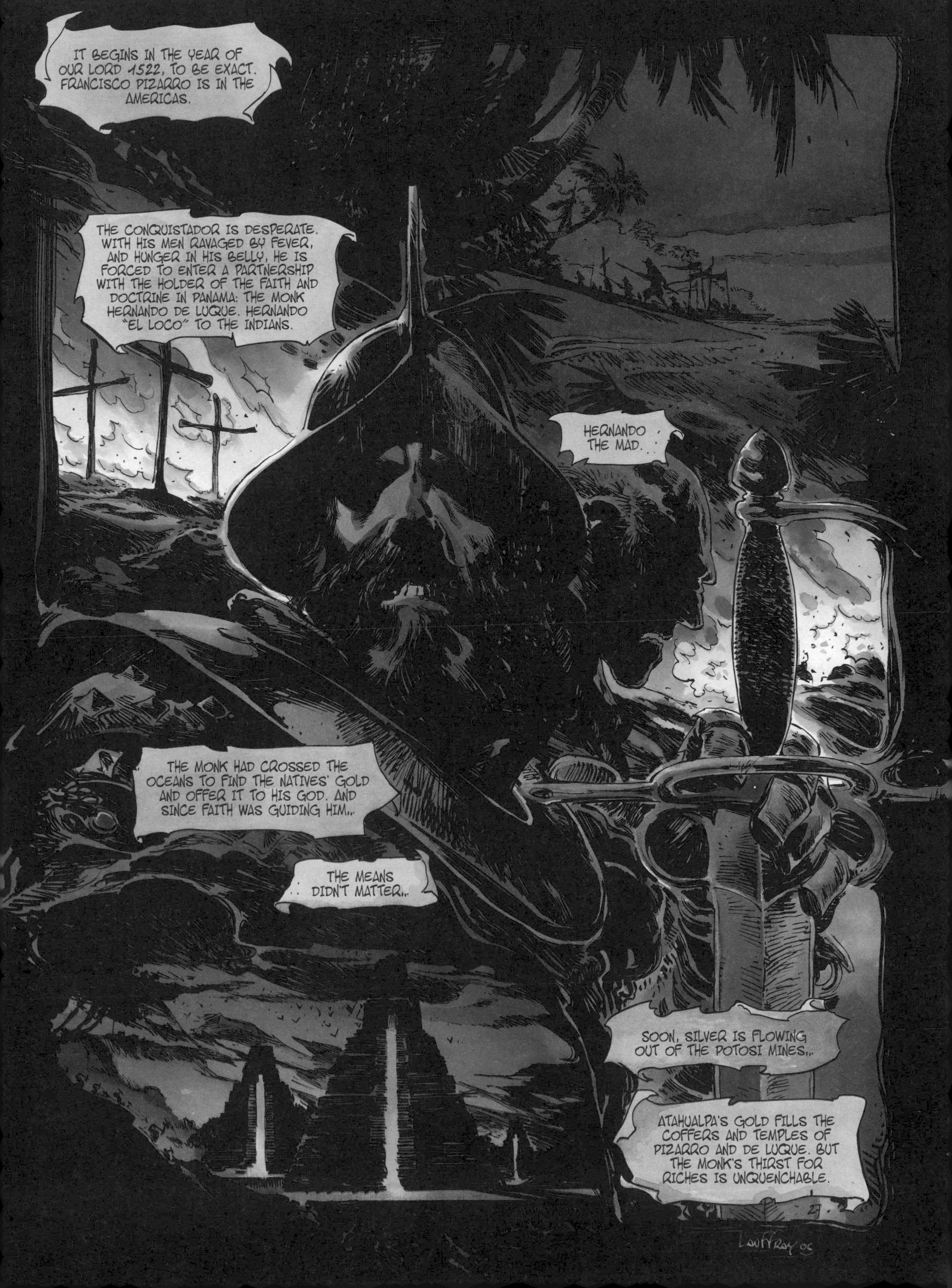
IT BEGINS IN THE YEAR OF OUR LORD 1522, TO BE EXACT. FRANCISCO PIZARRO IS IN THE AMERICAS.
THE CONQUISTADOR IS DESPERATE. WITH HIS MEN RAVAGED BY FEVER, AND HUNGER IN HIS BELLY, HE IS FORCED TO ENTER A PARTNERSHIP WITH THE HOLDER OF THE FAITH AND DOCTRINE IN PANAMA: THE MONK HERNANDO DE LUQUE. HERNANDO "EL LOCO" TO THE INDIANS.
HERNANDO THE MAD.
THE MONK HAD CROSSED THE OCEANS TO FIND THE NATIVES' GOLD AND OFFER IT TO HIS GOD. AND SINCE FAITH WAS GUIDING HIM...
THE MEANS DIDN'T MATTER...
SOON, SILVER IS FLOWING OUT OF THE POTOSI MINES...
ATAHUALPA'S GOLD FILLS THE COFFERS AND TEMPLES OF PIZARRO AND DE LUQUE. BUT THE MONK'S THIRST FOR RICHES IS UNQUENCHABLE.
27
LAUFFRAY 05

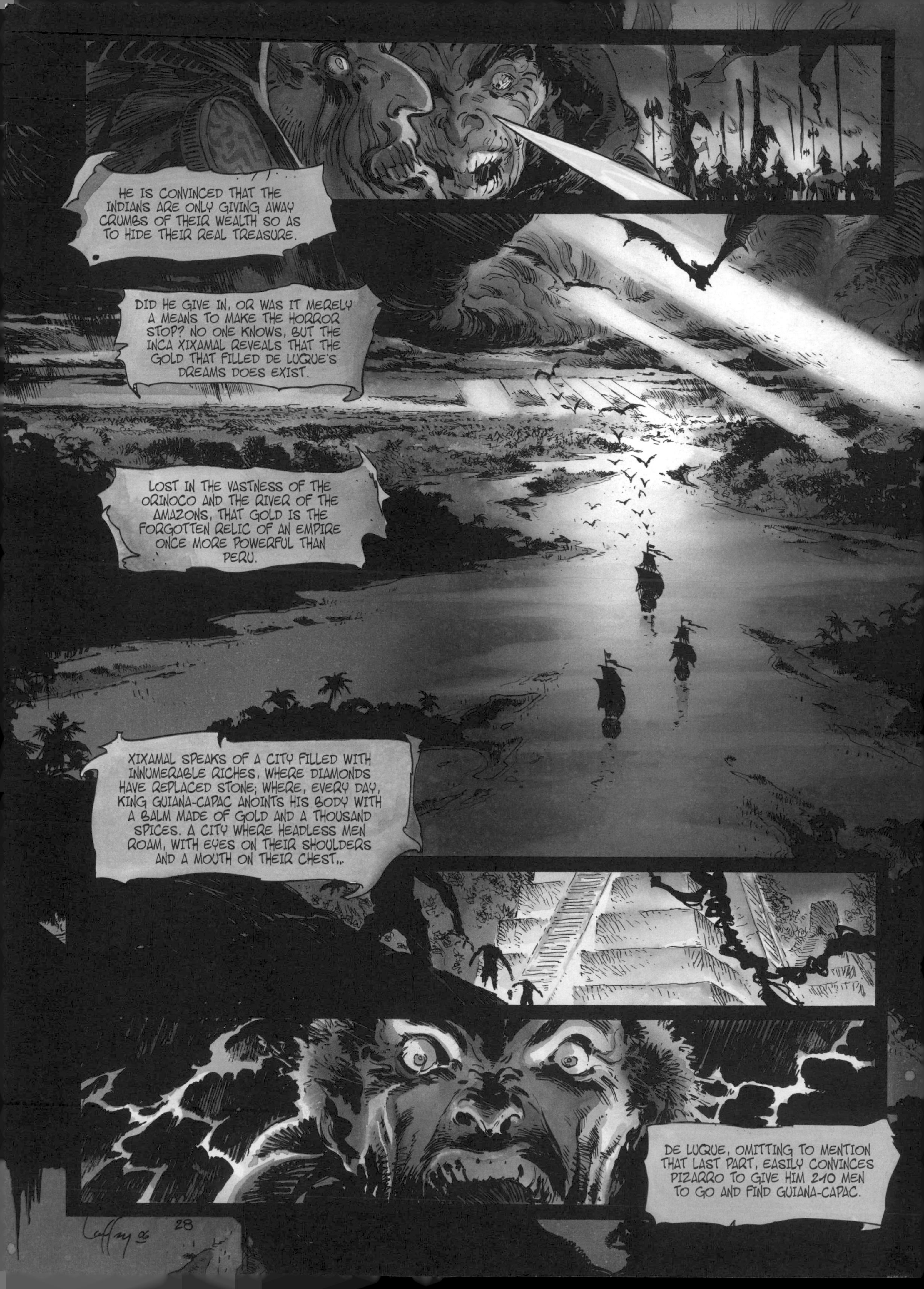
HE IS CONVINCED THAT THE INDIANS ARE ONLY GIVING AWAY CRUMBS OF THEIR WEALTH SO AS TO HIDE THEIR REAL TREASURE.
DID HE GIVE IN, OR WAS IT MERELY A MEANS TO MAKE THE HORROR STOP? NO ONE KNOWS, BUT THE INCA XIXAMAL REVEALS THAT THE GOLD THAT FILLED DE LUQUE'S DREAMS DOES EXIST.
LOST IN THE VASTNESS OF THE ORINOCO AND THE RIVER OF THE AMAZONS, THAT GOLD IS THE FORGOTTEN RELIC OF AN EMPIRE ONCE MORE POWERFUL THAN PERU.
XIXAMAL SPEAKS OF A CITY FILLED WITH INNUMERABLE RICHES, WHERE DIAMONDS HAVE REPLACED STONE; WHERE, EVERY DAY, KING GUIANA-CAPAC ANOINTS HIS BODY WITH A BALM MADE OF GOLD AND A THOUSAND SPICES. A CITY WHERE HEADLESS MEN ROAM, WITH EYES ON THEIR SHOULDERS AND A MOUTH ON THEIR CHEST...
DE LUQUE, OMITTING TO MENTION THAT LAST PART, EASILY CONVINCES PIZARRO TO GIVE HIM 210 MEN TO GO AND FIND GUIANA-CAPAC.
28

NONE EVER CAME BACK.

I DO NOT KNOW WHEN MY HUSBAND BECAME ENTHRALLED BY THIS STORY. BUT, THREE YEARS AGO, A SPANISH CATHOLIC PRIEST OFFERED HIM A MAYAN MAP— APPARENTLY IDENTICAL TO THE ONE USED BY DE LUQUE.

BYRON SOLD HALF OF MY LANDS TO PURCHASE THAT PARCHMENT. HE TOOK MONTHS DECIPHERING IT, THEN LEFT FOR THE AMERICAS. AT FIRST, I THOUGHT HE WAS MAD. THEN I HOPED HE WAS DEAD. I WAS WRONG; A LETTER FROM HIM JUST REACHED ME.

HE FOUND GUIANA-CAPAC.

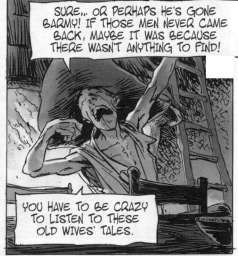

SURE... OR PERHAPS HE'S GONE BARMY! IF THOSE MEN NEVER CAME BACK, MAYBE IT WAS BECAUSE THERE WASN'T ANYTHING TO FIND!

YOU HAVE TO BE CRAZY TO LISTEN TO THESE OLD WIVES' TALES.

WHAT?! YOU WOULD CALL THEM CRAZY? JUAN DE SOLIS, WHO DISCOVERED THE ESTUARY OF LA PLATA? SEBASTIAN CABOT, WHO SAILED UP THE RIO DE LA PLATA AND THE PARAGUAY RIVER? WHAT OF JIMENEZ DE QUESADA, ANTONIO DE BERRI OR THE BASQUE DON LOPE DE AGUIRRE!?

THEY ALL BELIEVED IN ELDORADO.

AND HOW MANY OF THEM ENDED UP IN BITS INSIDE SOME SAVAGE'S BELLY?

COME NOW, MY FRIENDS! WE'LL PUT OUR DECISION TO THE VOTE LATER.

FOR THE MOMENT, LET'S SEE HOW WE CAN HELP OUT OUR DEAR LADY HASTINGS...

29-

CAPTAIN HASTINGS IS TO SECURE AND CHARTER A SHIP IN THE COMING DAYS. FIND A WAY TO BE HIRED AS PART OF THE CREW.

WAIT FOR THE EXPEDITION TO REACH GUIANA-CAPAC BEFORE YOU ATTEMPT ANYTHING. IT IS OUR ONLY CHANCE TO FULFIL THE OBJECTIVE OF OUR JOURNEY.

ONCE THERE, YOU WILL BE OUTNUMBERED. YOU WILL HAVE TO WORK DISCREETLY AND WITHOUT BLOODSHED.

WITH THESE CONDITION IN MIND, YOU WILL TAKE ANYTHING YOU WISH; SUCH WILL BE YOUR WAGES. HALF OF EVERYTHING WILL BE MINE. THEN YOU WILL TAKE ME BACK TO THE CONTINENT—AND WE WILL FORGET THAT OUR PATHS EVER CROSSED.

HMM... SHOULD DISCRETION NO LONGER BE AN OPTION, FOR YOUR HUSBAND OR ANY REBELLIOUS SOUL... WHAT SHALL WE DO?

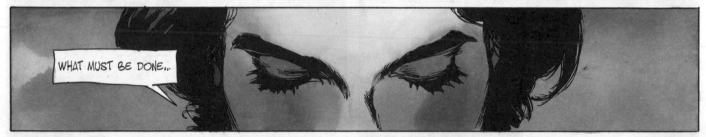

WHAT MUST BE DONE...

AND IF WE DECIDE FROM THE START TO DO THINGS OUR WAY, WHAT WILL YOU DO? SCOLD US?

I WILL DENOUNCE YOU, AND YOU WILL BE HANGED FROM THE YARDARM...

WHERE YOU'LL JOIN US!! AS FAR AS THE CAPTAIN IS CONCERNED, WE'LL BE TARRED WITH THE SAME BRUSH!

GOOD—I DO SO ENJOY YOUR COMPANY!

30

COME IN, DOCTOR. SIT DOWN.
STILL DEFENDING THE WIDOW AND THE ORPHAN, I SEE.
LADY HASTINGS IS COMPLETELY INSANE, SILVER. SHE HAS ABSOLUTELY NO IDEA WHAT SHE IS DOING. TURN DOWN HER OFFER.
YOU'VE ALWAYS BEEN A PUZZLE TO ME, DOCTOR. HOW MUCH TIME HAS PASSED, AGAIN..? 15 YEARS, 20 YEARS?..
THEN, OUT OF THAT DISTANT PAST, YOU COME TO ME IN THE COMPANY OF A YOUNG LADY. YOU ASK FOR MY ASSISTANCE IN THE MOST FASCINATING OF ENDEAVOURS...
AND NOW I HAVE TO TURN IT DOWN. DO EXPLAIN, WILL YOU?..
BESIDES, YOU SEEMED RATHER ENTHUSIASTIC TO ME EARLIER..
I... I WAS MERELY RESTORING HISTORICAL TRUTHS! MY COMING HERE WAS ONLY INTENDED TO DISCOURAGE A LADY FROM SEEKING IMPROPER THRILLS! I NEVER THOUGHT SHE WOULD GO THIS FAR.
FORTUNATELY, THERE'S STILL TIME TO STOP EVERYTHING.
ON THE CONTRARY, DOCTOR. IT'S MUCH TOO LATE FOR THAT. THIS DEAL WAS OFFERED TO ME FAIR AND SQUARE.
THIS LADY CAN COUNT ON LONG JOHN SILVER'S HELP.
MY TURN TO BE QUITE CLEAR, THEN, SILVER. IF YOU COME WITHIN A MILE OF THE SHIP, EXPECT TO BE WELCOMED BY AN ENTIRE GARRISON—ONE I WILL ALERT MYSELF!
I WILL NOT BE PARTY TO AN ACT OF PIRACY!
YOU KNOW I'M NOT BLUFFING.
GNN..
SILVER? SILVER?!
31 -

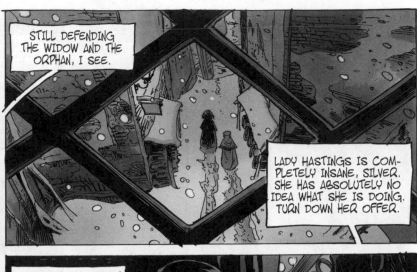

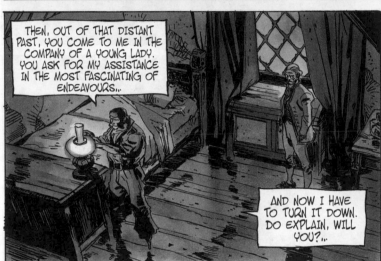

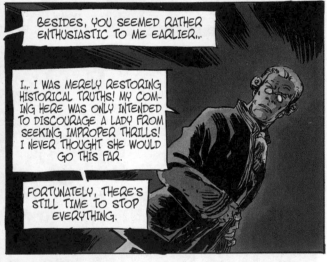

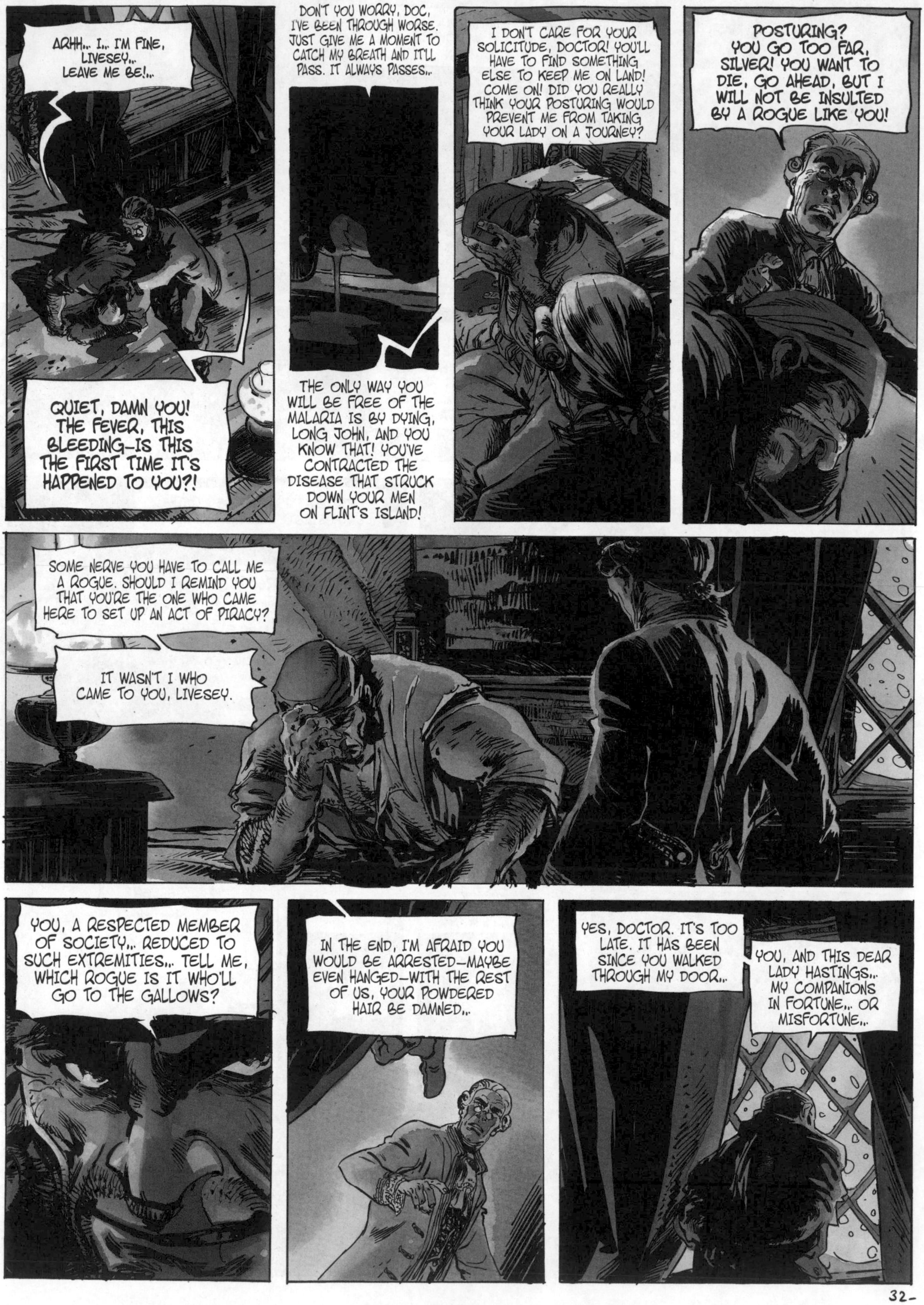
ARHH.. I.. I'M FINE, LIVESEY.. LEAVE ME BE!..
QUIET, DAMN YOU! THE FEVER, THIS BLEEDING—IS THIS THE FIRST TIME IT'S HAPPENED TO YOU?!
DON'T YOU WORRY, DOC, I'VE BEEN THROUGH WORSE. JUST GIVE ME A MOMENT TO CATCH MY BREATH AND IT'LL PASS. IT ALWAYS PASSES..
THE ONLY WAY YOU WILL BE FREE OF THE MALARIA IS BY DYING, LONG JOHN, AND YOU KNOW THAT! YOU'VE CONTRACTED THE DISEASE THAT STRUCK DOWN YOUR MEN ON FLINT'S ISLAND!
I DON'T CARE FOR YOUR SOLICITUDE, DOCTOR! YOU'LL HAVE TO FIND SOMETHING ELSE TO KEEP ME ON LAND! COME ON! DID YOU REALLY THINK YOUR POSTURING WOULD PREVENT ME FROM TAKING YOUR LADY ON A JOURNEY?
POSTURING? YOU GO TOO FAR, SILVER! YOU WANT TO DIE, GO AHEAD, BUT I WILL NOT BE INSULTED BY A ROGUE LIKE YOU!
SOME NERVE YOU HAVE TO CALL ME A ROGUE. SHOULD I REMIND YOU THAT YOU'RE THE ONE WHO CAME HERE TO SET UP AN ACT OF PIRACY?
IT WASN'T I WHO CAME TO YOU, LIVESEY.
YOU, A RESPECTED MEMBER OF SOCIETY.. REDUCED TO SUCH EXTREMITIES.. TELL ME, WHICH ROGUE IS IT WHO'LL GO TO THE GALLOWS?
IN THE END, I'M AFRAID YOU WOULD BE ARRESTED—MAYBE EVEN HANGED—WITH THE REST OF US, YOUR POWDERED HAIR BE DAMNED..
YES, DOCTOR. IT'S TOO LATE. IT HAS BEEN SINCE YOU WALKED THROUGH MY DOOR..
YOU, AND THIS DEAR LADY HASTINGS.. MY COMPANIONS IN FORTUNE.. OR MISFORTUNE..
32-

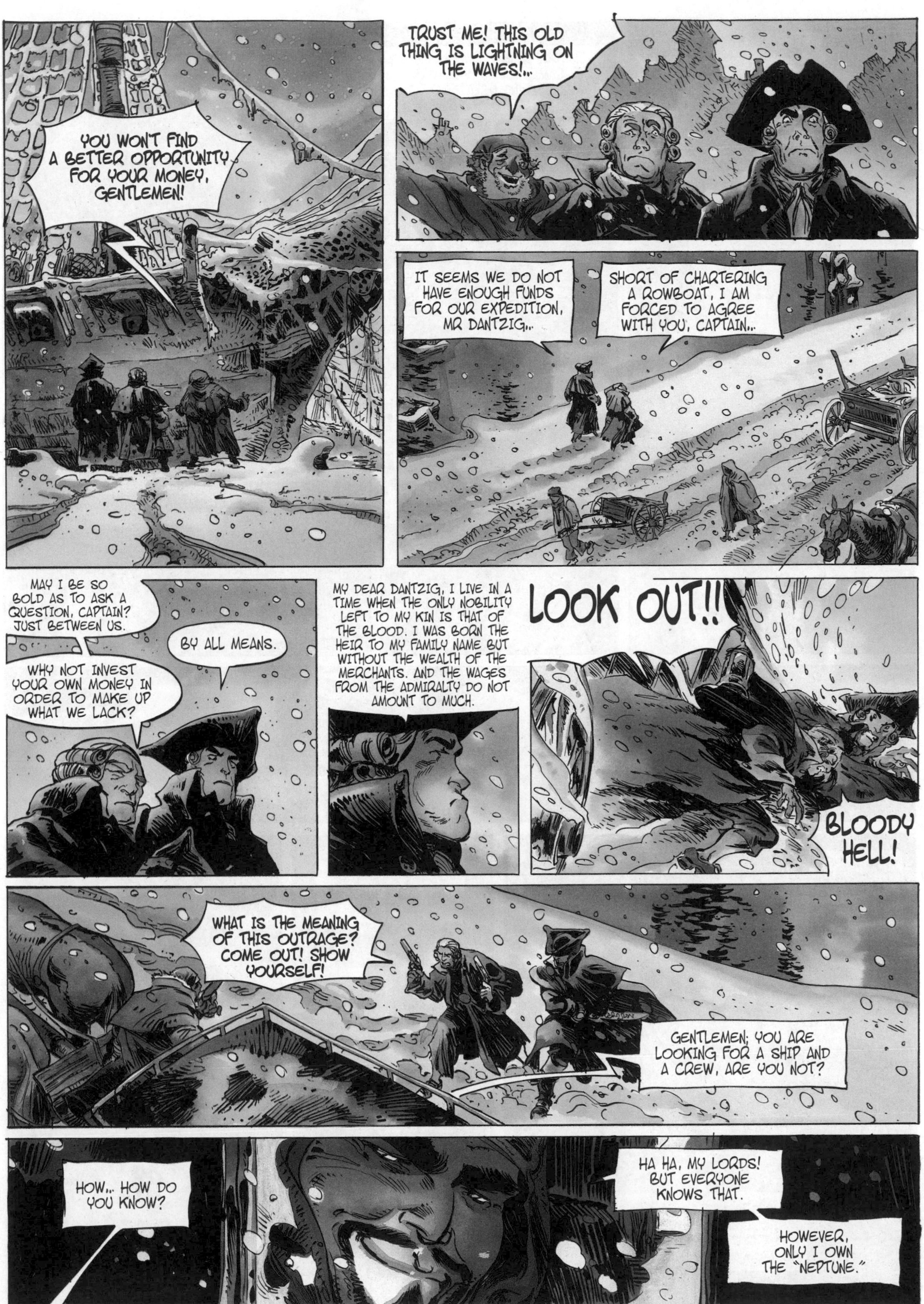
YOU WON'T FIND A BETTER OPPORTUNITY FOR YOUR MONEY, GENTLEMEN!
TRUST ME! THIS OLD THING IS LIGHTNING ON THE WAVES!..
IT SEEMS WE DO NOT HAVE ENOUGH FUNDS FOR OUR EXPEDITION, MR DANTZIG..
SHORT OF CHARTERING A ROWBOAT, I AM FORCED TO AGREE WITH YOU, CAPTAIN..
MAY I BE SO BOLD AS TO ASK A QUESTION, CAPTAIN? JUST BETWEEN US.
BY ALL MEANS.
WHY NOT INVEST YOUR OWN MONEY IN ORDER TO MAKE UP WHAT WE LACK?
MY DEAR DANTZIG, I LIVE IN A TIME WHEN THE ONLY NOBILITY LEFT TO MY KIN IS THAT OF THE BLOOD. I WAS BORN THE HEIR TO MY FAMILY NAME BUT WITHOUT THE WEALTH OF THE MERCHANTS. AND THE WAGES FROM THE ADMIRALTY DO NOT AMOUNT TO MUCH.
LOOK OUT!!
BLOODY HELL!
WHAT IS THE MEANING OF THIS OUTRAGE? COME OUT! SHOW YOURSELF!
GENTLEMEN; YOU ARE LOOKING FOR A SHIP AND A CREW, ARE YOU NOT?
HOW.. HOW DO YOU KNOW?
HA HA, MY LORDS! BUT EVERYONE KNOWS THAT.
HOWEVER, ONLY I OWN THE "NEPTUNE."
33-

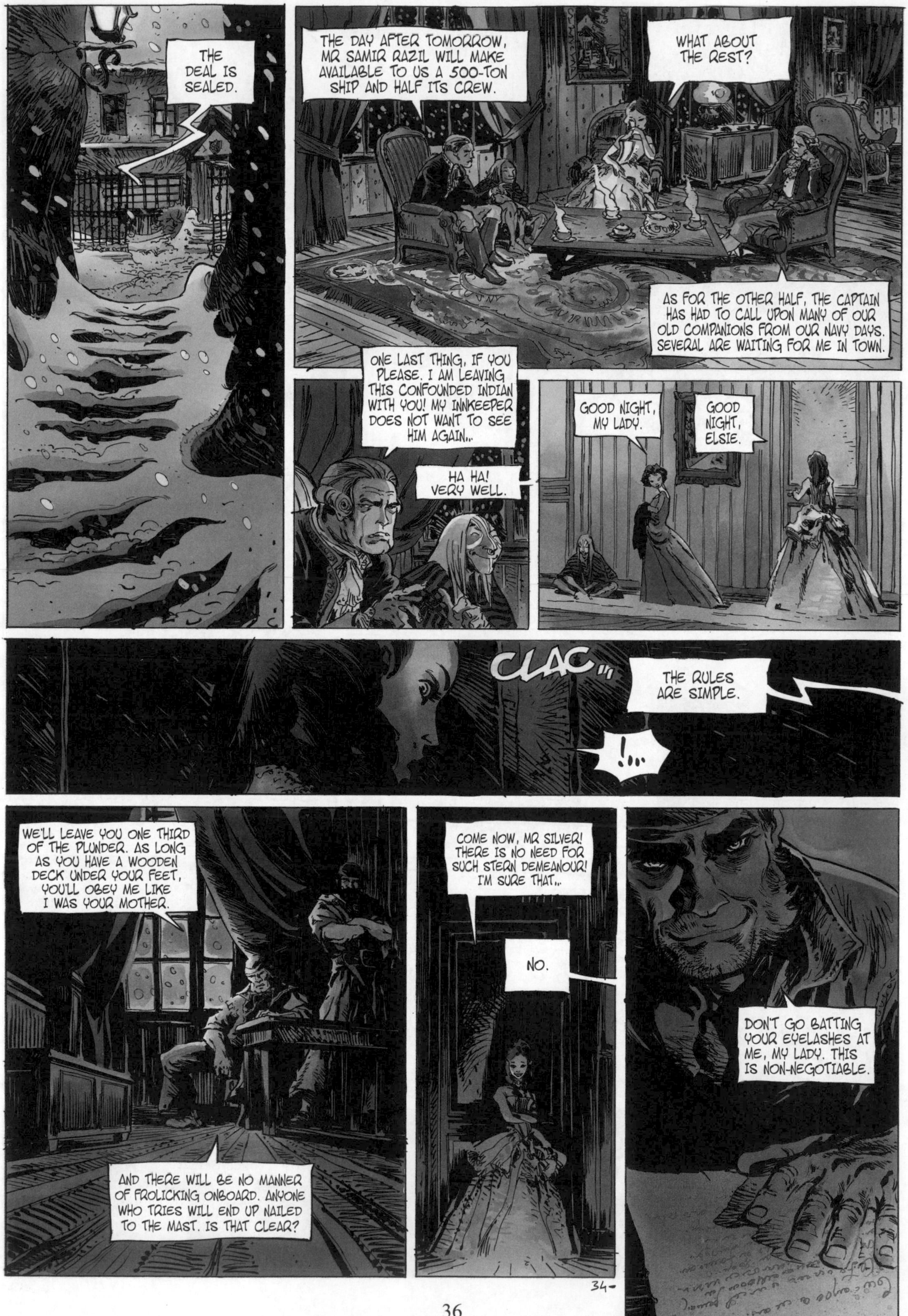
THE DEAL IS SEALED.
THE DAY AFTER TOMORROW, MR SAMIR RAZIL WILL MAKE AVAILABLE TO US A 500-TON SHIP AND HALF ITS CREW.
WHAT ABOUT THE REST?
AS FOR THE OTHER HALF, THE CAPTAIN HAS HAD TO CALL UPON MANY OF OUR OLD COMPANIONS FROM OUR NAVY DAYS. SEVERAL ARE WAITING FOR ME IN TOWN.
ONE LAST THING, IF YOU PLEASE. I AM LEAVING THIS CONFOUNDED INDIAN WITH YOU! MY INNKEEPER DOES NOT WANT TO SEE HIM AGAIN...
HA HA! VERY WELL.
GOOD NIGHT, MY LADY.
GOOD NIGHT, ELSIE.
CLAC...
THE RULES ARE SIMPLE.
!...
WE'LL LEAVE YOU ONE THIRD OF THE PLUNDER. AS LONG AS YOU HAVE A WOODEN DECK UNDER YOUR FEET, YOU'LL OBEY ME LIKE I WAS YOUR MOTHER.
AND THERE WILL BE NO MANNER OF FROLICKING ONBOARD. ANYONE WHO TRIES WILL END UP NAILED TO THE MAST. IS THAT CLEAR?
COME NOW, MR SILVER! THERE IS NO NEED FOR SUCH STERN DEMEANOUR! I'M SURE THAT...
NO.
DON'T GO BATTING YOUR EYELASHES AT ME, MY LADY. THIS IS NON-NEGOTIABLE.

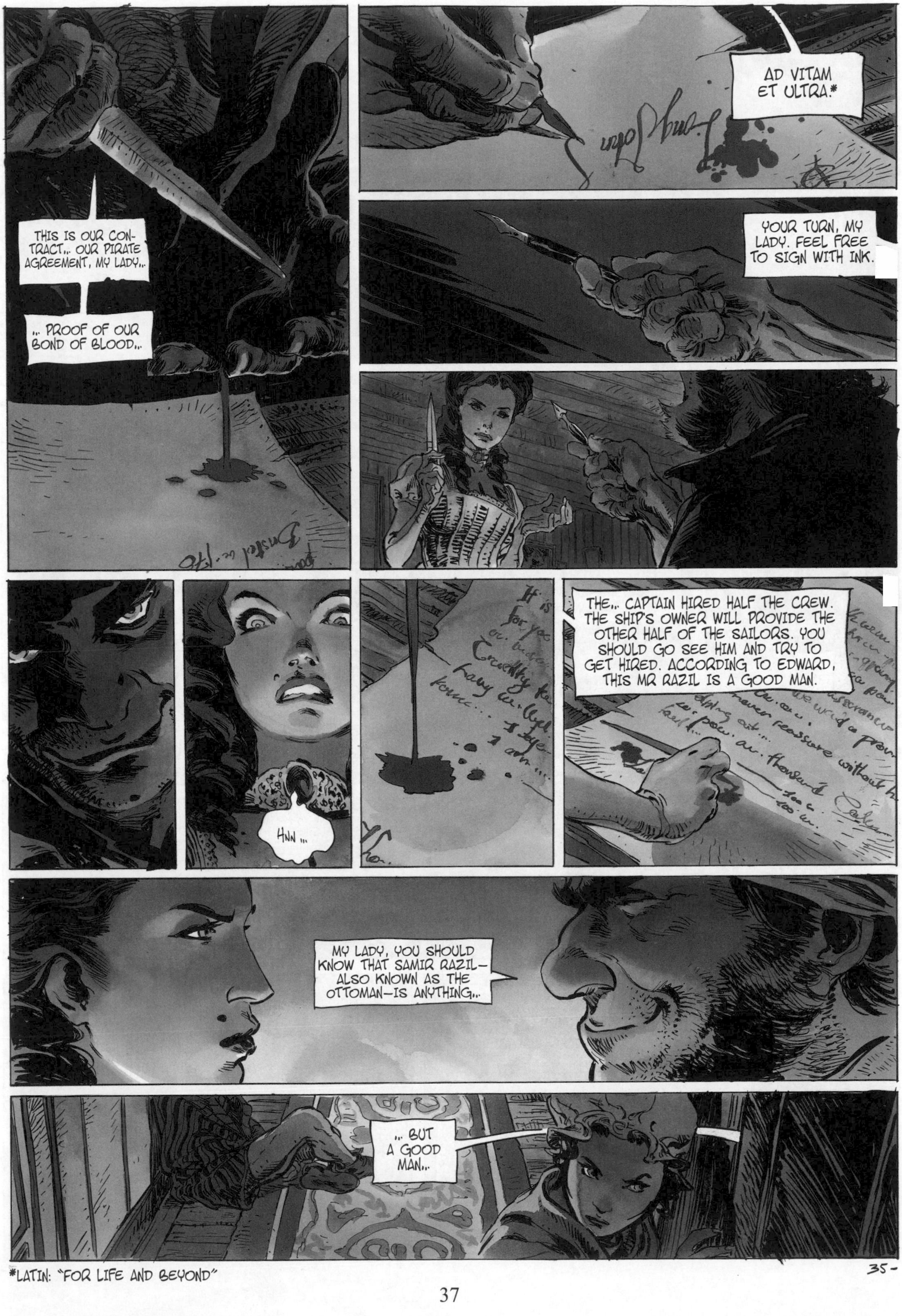
THIS IS OUR CONTRACT... OUR PIRATE AGREEMENT, MY LADY...
... PROOF OF OUR BOND OF BLOOD...
AD VITAM ET ULTRA.*
YOUR TURN, MY LADY. FEEL FREE TO SIGN WITH INK.
HNN ...
THE... CAPTAIN HIRED HALF THE CREW. THE SHIP'S OWNER WILL PROVIDE THE OTHER HALF OF THE SAILORS. YOU SHOULD GO SEE HIM AND TRY TO GET HIRED. ACCORDING TO EDWARD, THIS MR RAZIL IS A GOOD MAN.
MY LADY, YOU SHOULD KNOW THAT SAMIR RAZIL–ALSO KNOWN AS THE OTTOMAN–IS ANYTHING...
... BUT A GOOD MAN...

*LATIN: "FOR LIFE AND BEYOND"

MY GOD, SHE DID IT.

SHE SIGNED.

PSST...

GOOD EVENING, DOC...

SAY, THIS IS A NASTY PART OF TOWN. NOT GOOD FOR MUCH EXCEPT ATTRACTING ALL SORTS OF UNPLEASANTNESS.

I HAVE ALREADY WARNED SILVER, MR BONNET. HE KNOWS WHAT TO EXPECT. IF YOU ARE HERE TO KILL ME, DO IT NOW. BECAUSE I INTEND TO GO TO THE KING'S REPRESENTATIVE HERE AND WARN HIM OF WHAT IS TAKING PLACE.

NOW, NOW, DOCTOR. SILVER'S VERY FOND OF YOU. BESIDES, IF ANYTHING HAPPENED TO A MAN SUCH AS YOU... THERE WOULD BE QUESTIONS, AN INQUIRY. IT WOULDN'T LOOK RIGHT, JUST BEFORE WE SET SAIL.

ON THE OTHER HAND, IF THE KING'S MEN WERE TO LEARN ABOUT OUR BUSINESS, I WOULDN'T GIVE TWO SHILLINGS FOR YOUR CHANCES...

... OR THOSE OF THE PRETTY LADY.

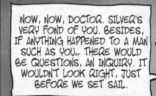

GO ON, DOC. BE A GOOD SUBJECT. AND TOMORROW, YOU WILL BE BACK IN YOUR COTTAGE-YOUR CONSCIENCE AT PEACE, YOUR DUTY DONE.

WHILE WE ROT AWAY IN IRON CAGES, IN THE COMPANY OF THIS DEAR FRIEND YOU SO KINDLY INTRODUCED US TO.

36

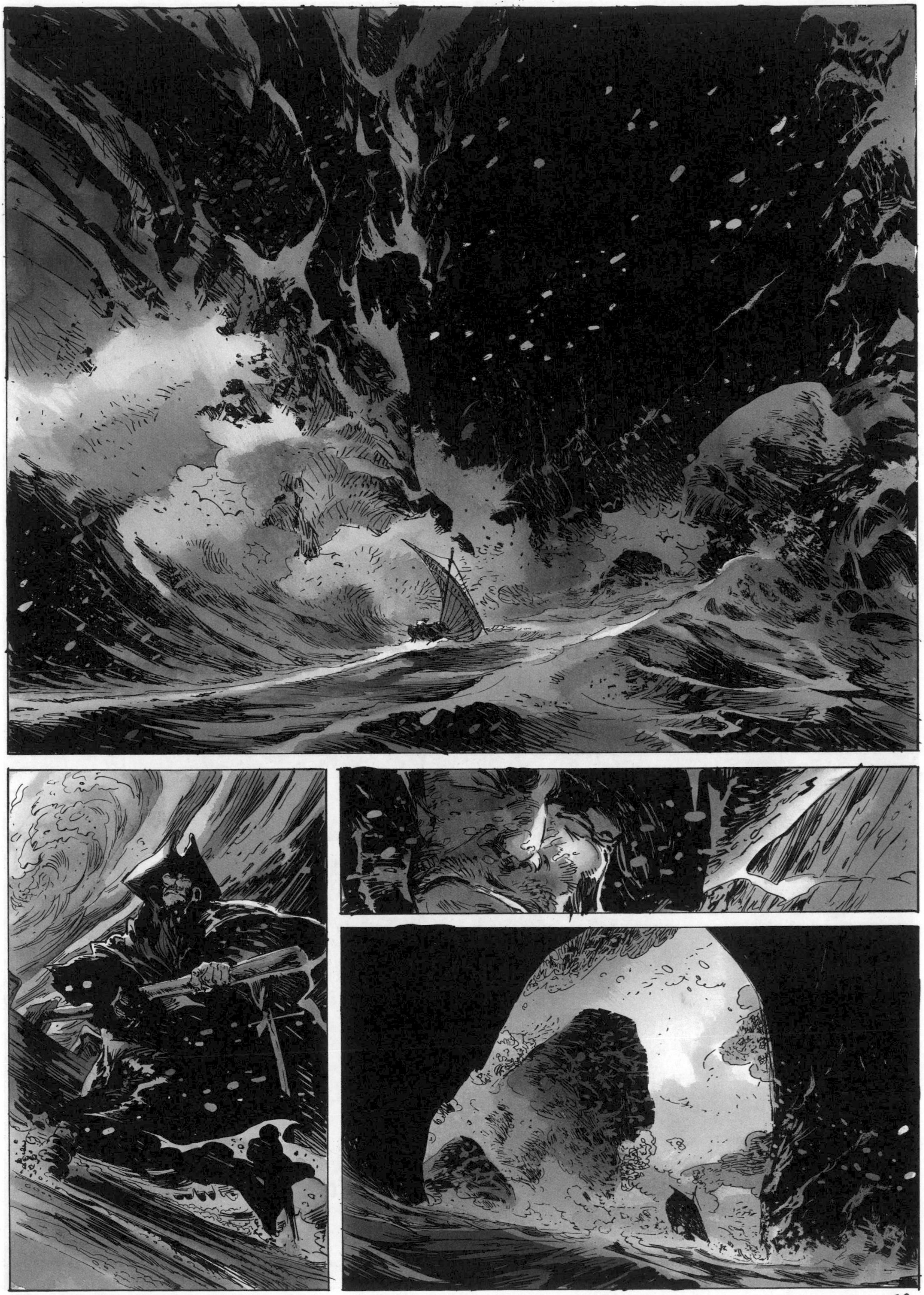

37-

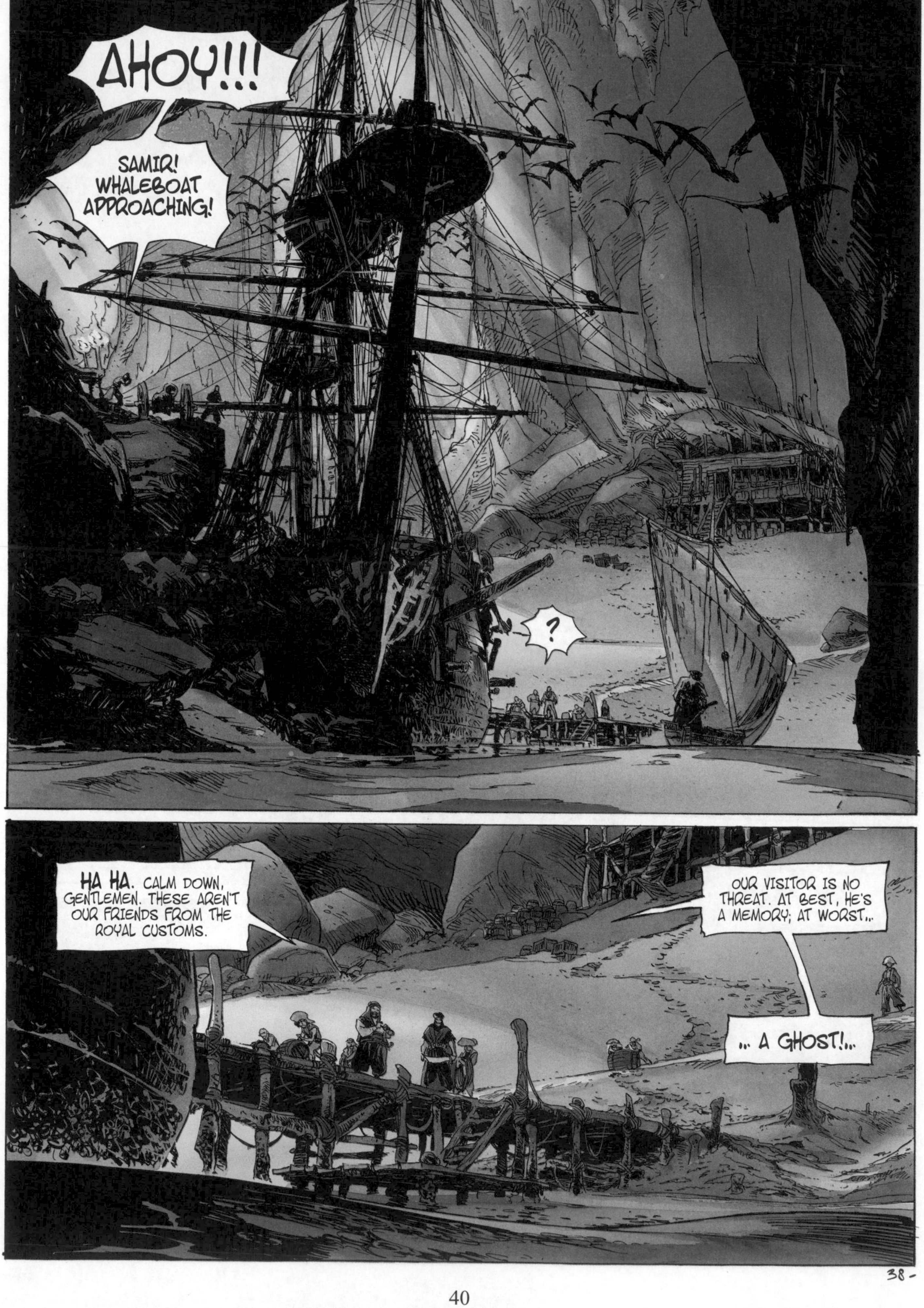
AHOY!!!
SAMIR! WHALEBOAT APPROACHING!
?
HA HA. CALM DOWN, GENTLEMEN. THESE AREN'T OUR FRIENDS FROM THE ROYAL CUSTOMS.
OUR VISITOR IS NO THREAT. AT BEST, HE'S A MEMORY; AT WORST...
... A GHOST!...

38-

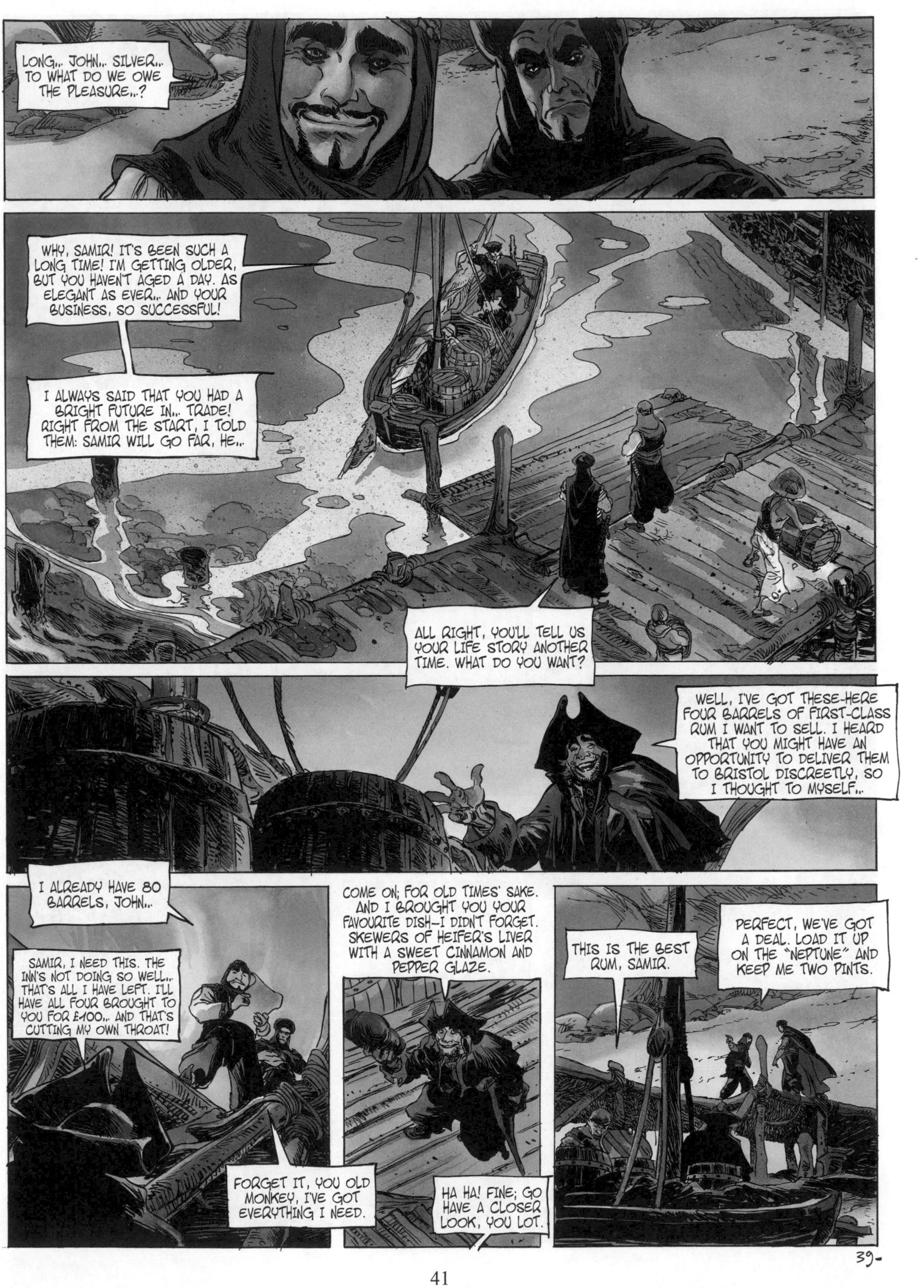
LONG... JOHN... SILVER... TO WHAT DO WE OWE THE PLEASURE...?
WHY, SAMIR! IT'S BEEN SUCH A LONG TIME! I'M GETTING OLDER, BUT YOU HAVEN'T AGED A DAY. AS ELEGANT AS EVER... AND YOUR BUSINESS, SO SUCCESSFUL!
I ALWAYS SAID THAT YOU HAD A BRIGHT FUTURE IN... TRADE! RIGHT FROM THE START, I TOLD THEM: SAMIR WILL GO FAR, HE...
ALL RIGHT, YOU'LL TELL US YOUR LIFE STORY ANOTHER TIME. WHAT DO YOU WANT?
WELL, I'VE GOT THESE-HERE FOUR BARRELS OF FIRST-CLASS RUM I WANT TO SELL. I HEARD THAT YOU MIGHT HAVE AN OPPORTUNITY TO DELIVER THEM TO BRISTOL DISCREETLY, SO I THOUGHT TO MYSELF...
I ALREADY HAVE 80 BARRELS, JOHN...
SAMIR, I NEED THIS. THE INN'S NOT DOING SO WELL... THAT'S ALL I HAVE LEFT. I'LL HAVE ALL FOUR BROUGHT TO YOU FOR £100... AND THAT'S CUTTING MY OWN THROAT!
FORGET IT, YOU OLD MONKEY, I'VE GOT EVERYTHING I NEED.
COME ON; FOR OLD TIMES' SAKE. AND I BROUGHT YOU YOUR FAVOURITE DISH–I DIDN'T FORGET. SKEWERS OF HEIFER'S LIVER WITH A SWEET CINNAMON AND PEPPER GLAZE.
HA HA! FINE; GO HAVE A CLOSER LOOK, YOU LOT.
THIS IS THE BEST RUM, SAMIR.
PERFECT, WE'VE GOT A DEAL. LOAD IT UP ON THE "NEPTUNE" AND KEEP ME TWO PINTS.
39-

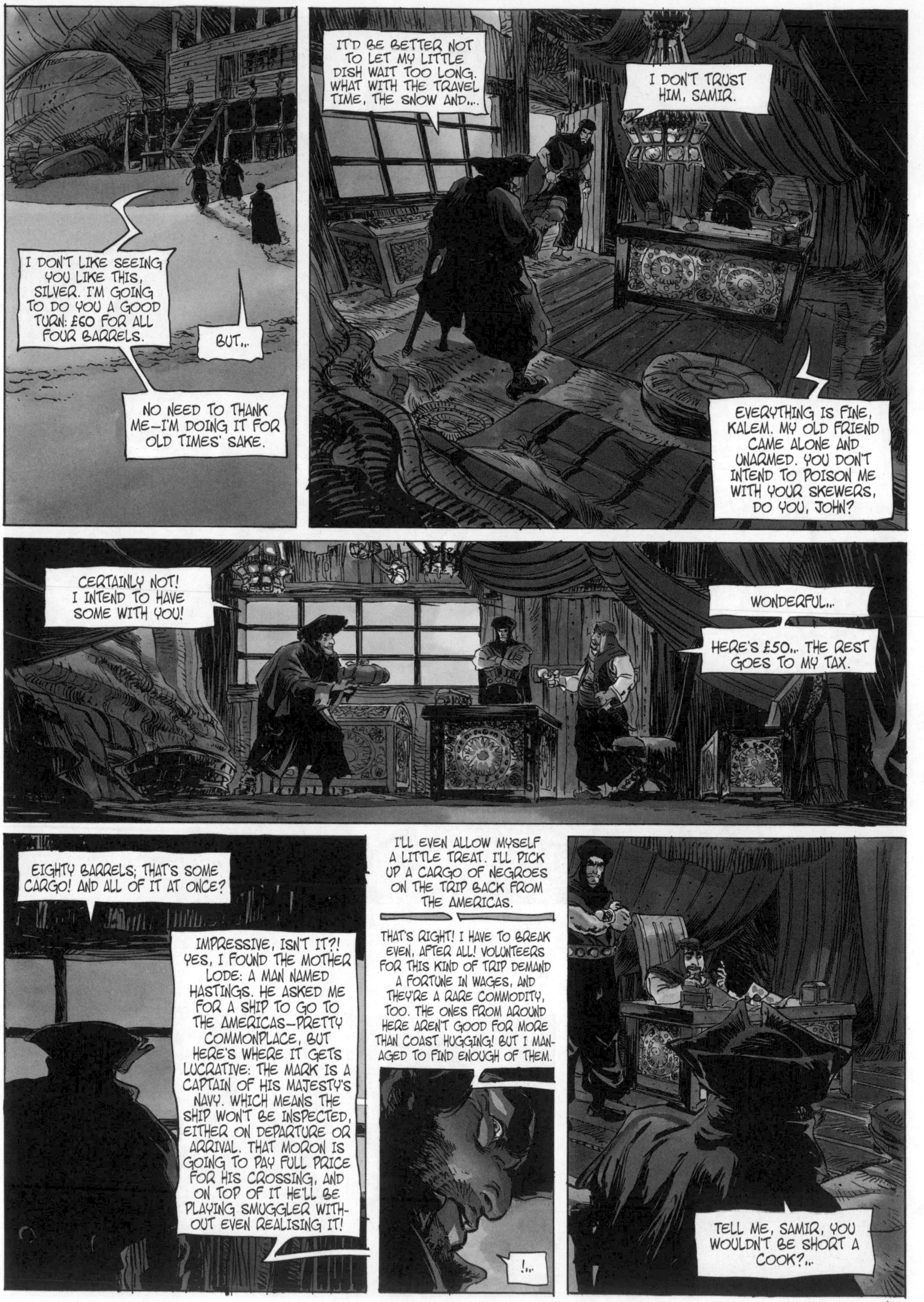
I DON'T LIKE SEEING YOU LIKE THIS, SILVER. I'M GOING TO DO YOU A GOOD TURN: £60 FOR ALL FOUR BARRELS.
BUT...
NO NEED TO THANK ME—I'M DOING IT FOR OLD TIMES' SAKE.
IT'D BE BETTER NOT TO LET MY LITTLE DISH WAIT TOO LONG. WHAT WITH THE TRAVEL TIME, THE SNOW AND...
I DON'T TRUST HIM, SAMIR.
EVERYTHING IS FINE, KALEM. MY OLD FRIEND CAME ALONE AND UNARMED. YOU DON'T INTEND TO POISON ME WITH YOUR SKEWERS, DO YOU, JOHN?
CERTAINLY NOT! I INTEND TO HAVE SOME WITH YOU!
WONDERFUL...
HERE'S £50... THE REST GOES TO MY TAX.
EIGHTY BARRELS; THAT'S SOME CARGO! AND ALL OF IT AT ONCE?
IMPRESSIVE, ISN'T IT?! YES, I FOUND THE MOTHER LODE: A MAN NAMED HASTINGS. HE ASKED ME FOR A SHIP TO GO TO THE AMERICAS—PRETTY COMMONPLACE, BUT HERE'S WHERE IT GETS LUCRATIVE: THE MARK IS A CAPTAIN OF HIS MAJESTY'S NAVY. WHICH MEANS THE SHIP WON'T BE INSPECTED, EITHER ON DEPARTURE OR ARRIVAL. THAT MORON IS GOING TO PAY FULL PRICE FOR HIS CROSSING, AND ON TOP OF IT HE'LL BE PLAYING SMUGGLER WITH-OUT EVEN REALISING IT!
I'LL EVEN ALLOW MYSELF A LITTLE TREAT. I'LL PICK UP A CARGO OF NEGROES ON THE TRIP BACK FROM THE AMERICAS.
THAT'S RIGHT! I HAVE TO BREAK EVEN, AFTER ALL! VOLUNTEERS FOR THIS KIND OF TRIP DEMAND A FORTUNE IN WAGES, AND THEY'RE A RARE COMMODITY, TOO. THE ONES FROM AROUND HERE AREN'T GOOD FOR MORE THAN COAST HUGGING! BUT I MAN-AGED TO FIND ENOUGH OF THEM.
!...
TELL ME, SAMIR, YOU WOULDN'T BE SHORT A COOK?...

40-

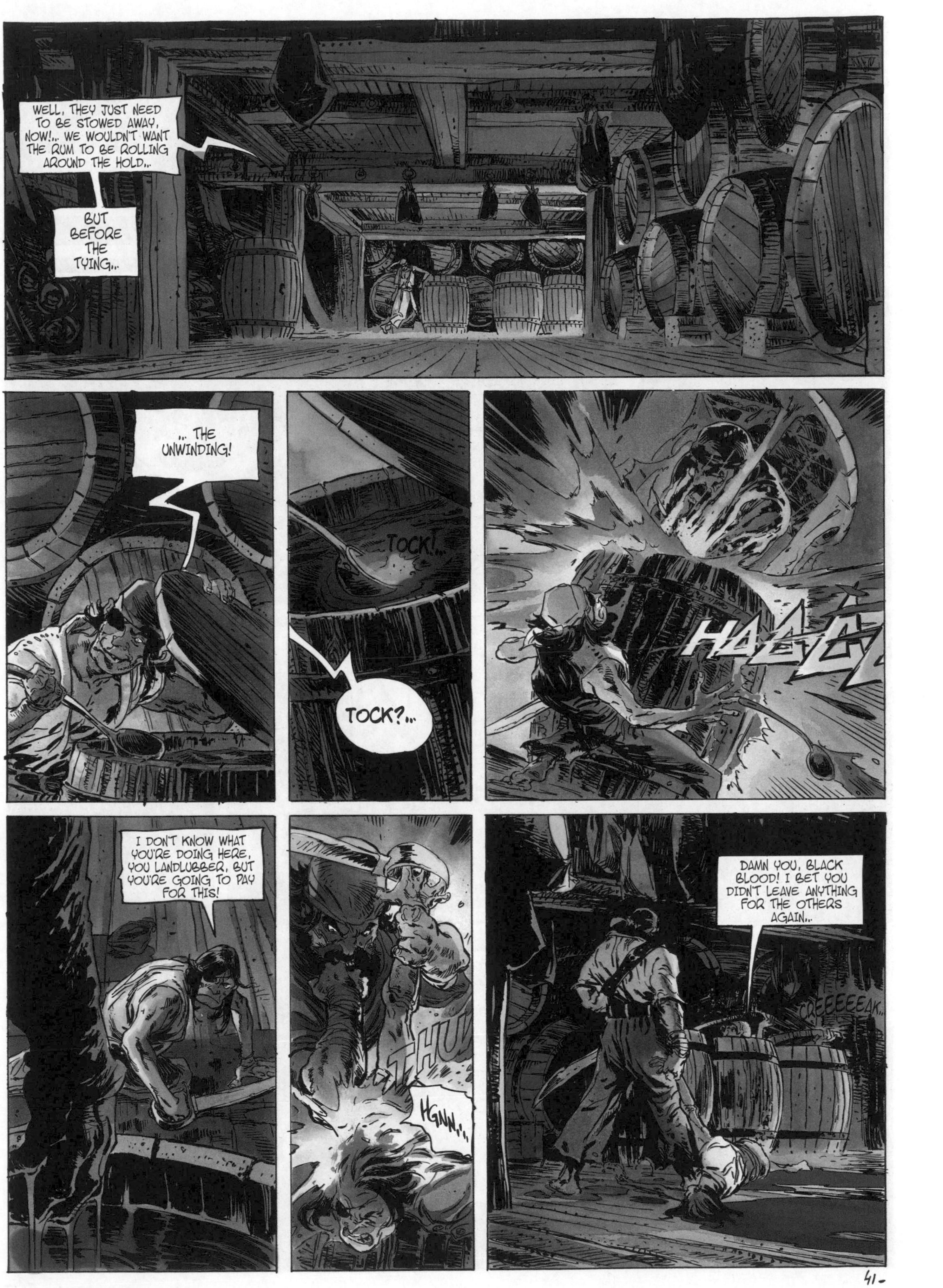

WELL, THEY JUST NEED TO BE STOWED AWAY, NOW!.. WE WOULDN'T WANT THE RUM TO BE ROLLING AROUND THE HOLD..
BUT BEFORE THE TYING..
.. THE UNWINDING!
TOCK!..
TOCK?..
I DON'T KNOW WHAT YOU'RE DOING HERE, YOU LANDLUBBER, BUT YOU'RE GOING TO PAY FOR THIS!
HGNN..
DAMN YOU, BLACK BLOOD! I BET YOU DIDN'T LEAVE ANYTHING FOR THE OTHERS AGAIN..
CREEEEEAK..
41-

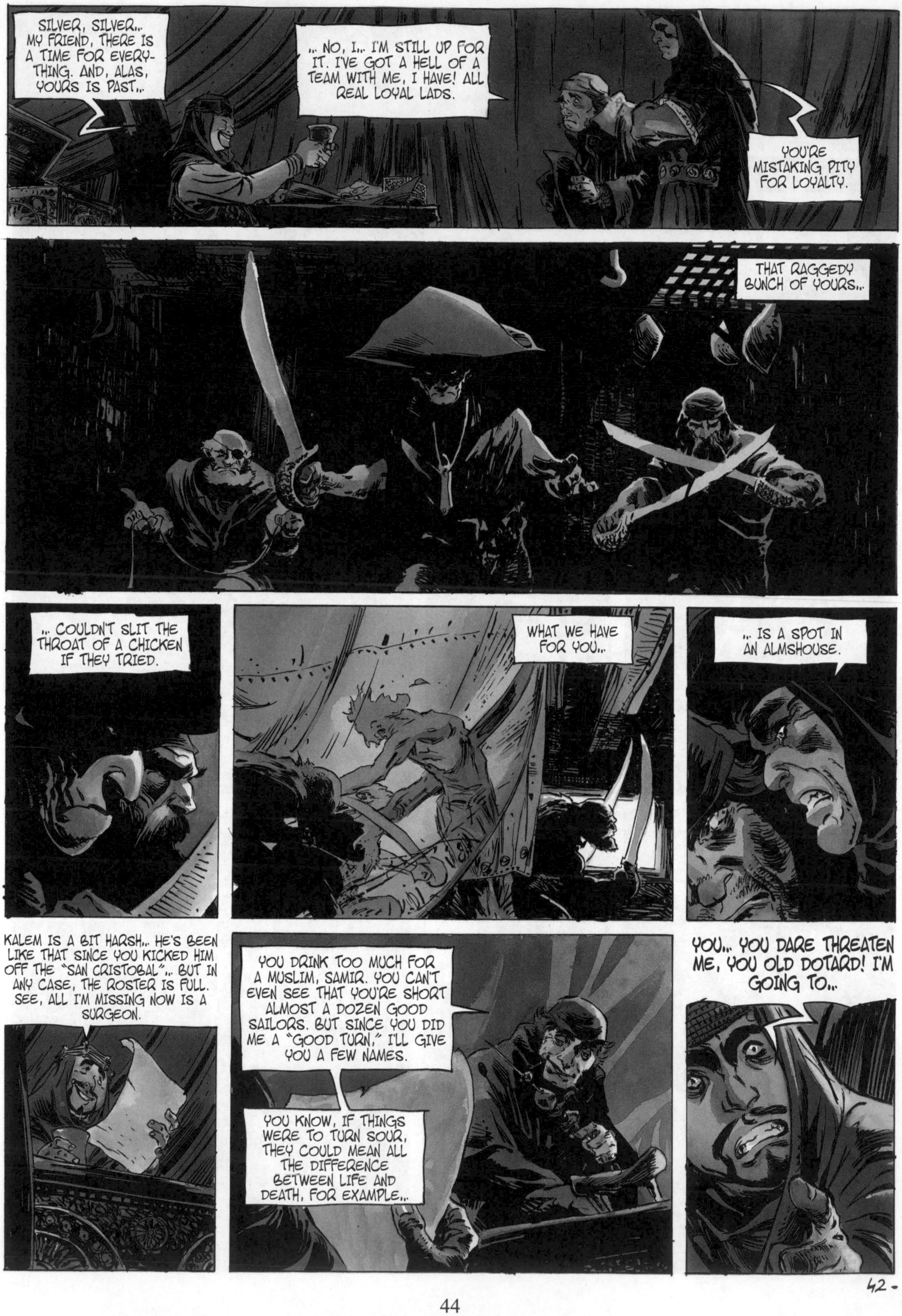

SILVER, SILVER.. MY FRIEND, THERE IS A TIME FOR EVERYTHING. AND, ALAS, YOURS IS PAST..
.. NO, I.. I'M STILL UP FOR IT. I'VE GOT A HELL OF A TEAM WITH ME, I HAVE! ALL REAL LOYAL LADS.
YOU'RE MISTAKING PITY FOR LOYALTY.
THAT RAGGEDY BUNCH OF YOURS..
.. COULDN'T SLIT THE THROAT OF A CHICKEN IF THEY TRIED.
WHAT WE HAVE FOR YOU..
.. IS A SPOT IN AN ALMSHOUSE.
KALEM IS A BIT HARSH.. HE'S BEEN LIKE THAT SINCE YOU KICKED HIM OFF THE "SAN CRISTOBAL".. BUT IN ANY CASE, THE ROSTER IS FULL. SEE, ALL I'M MISSING NOW IS A SURGEON.
YOU DRINK TOO MUCH FOR A MUSLIM, SAMIR. YOU CAN'T EVEN SEE THAT YOU'RE SHORT ALMOST A DOZEN GOOD SAILORS. BUT SINCE YOU DID ME A "GOOD TURN," I'LL GIVE YOU A FEW NAMES.
YOU KNOW, IF THINGS WERE TO TURN SOUR, THEY COULD MEAN ALL THE DIFFERENCE BETWEEN LIFE AND DEATH, FOR EXAMPLE..
YOU.. YOU DARE THREATEN ME, YOU OLD DOTARD! I'M GOING TO..
42 -

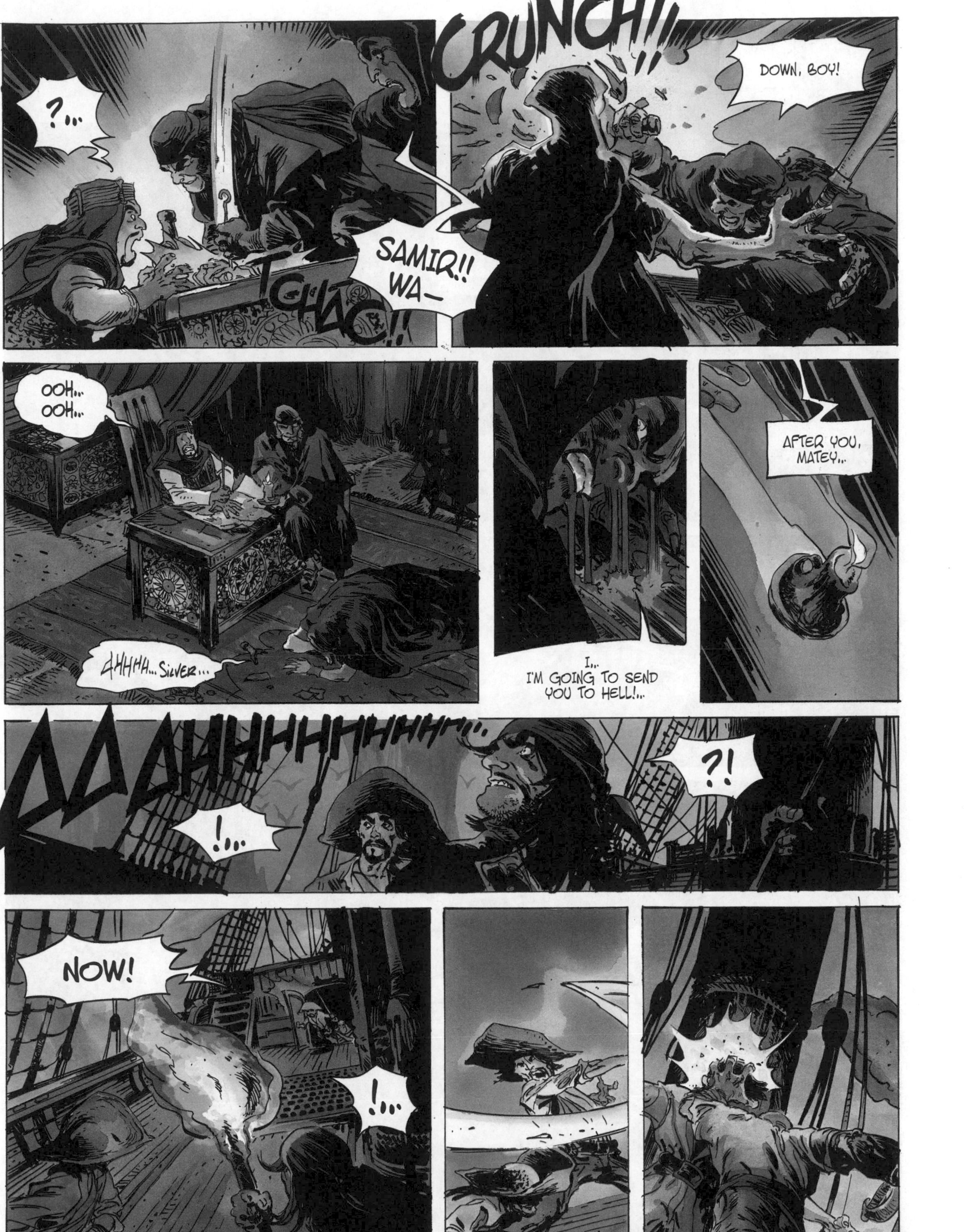
?...
CRUNCH!!!
DOWN, BOY!
SAMIR!! WA–
TCHAC!!
OOH... OOH...
AHHHH... SILVER...
I... I'M GOING TO SEND YOU TO HELL!...
AFTER YOU, MATEY...
AAAHHHHHHHH...
?!
!...
NOW!
!...
43-

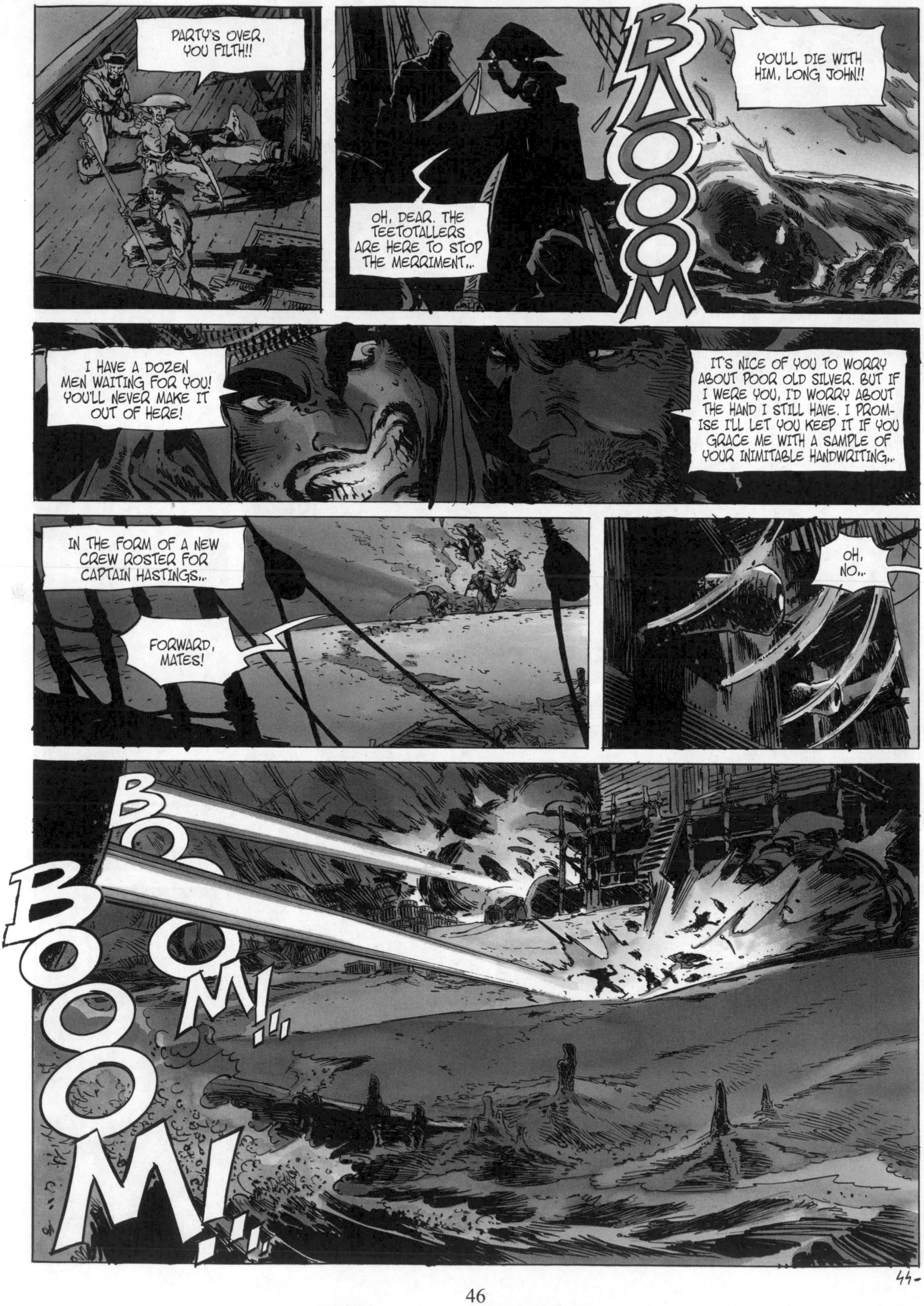
PARTY'S OVER, YOU FILTH!!
OH, DEAR. THE TEETOTALLERS ARE HERE TO STOP THE MERRIMENT...
BROOOOM
YOU'LL DIE WITH HIM, LONG JOHN!!
I HAVE A DOZEN MEN WAITING FOR YOU! YOU'LL NEVER MAKE IT OUT OF HERE!
IT'S NICE OF YOU TO WORRY ABOUT POOR OLD SILVER. BUT IF I WERE YOU, I'D WORRY ABOUT THE HAND I STILL HAVE. I PROMISE I'LL LET YOU KEEP IT IF YOU GRACE ME WITH A SAMPLE OF YOUR INIMITABLE HANDWRITING...
IN THE FORM OF A NEW CREW ROSTER FOR CAPTAIN HASTINGS...
FORWARD, MATES!
OH, NO...
BOOOM!!!
BOOOOM!!!

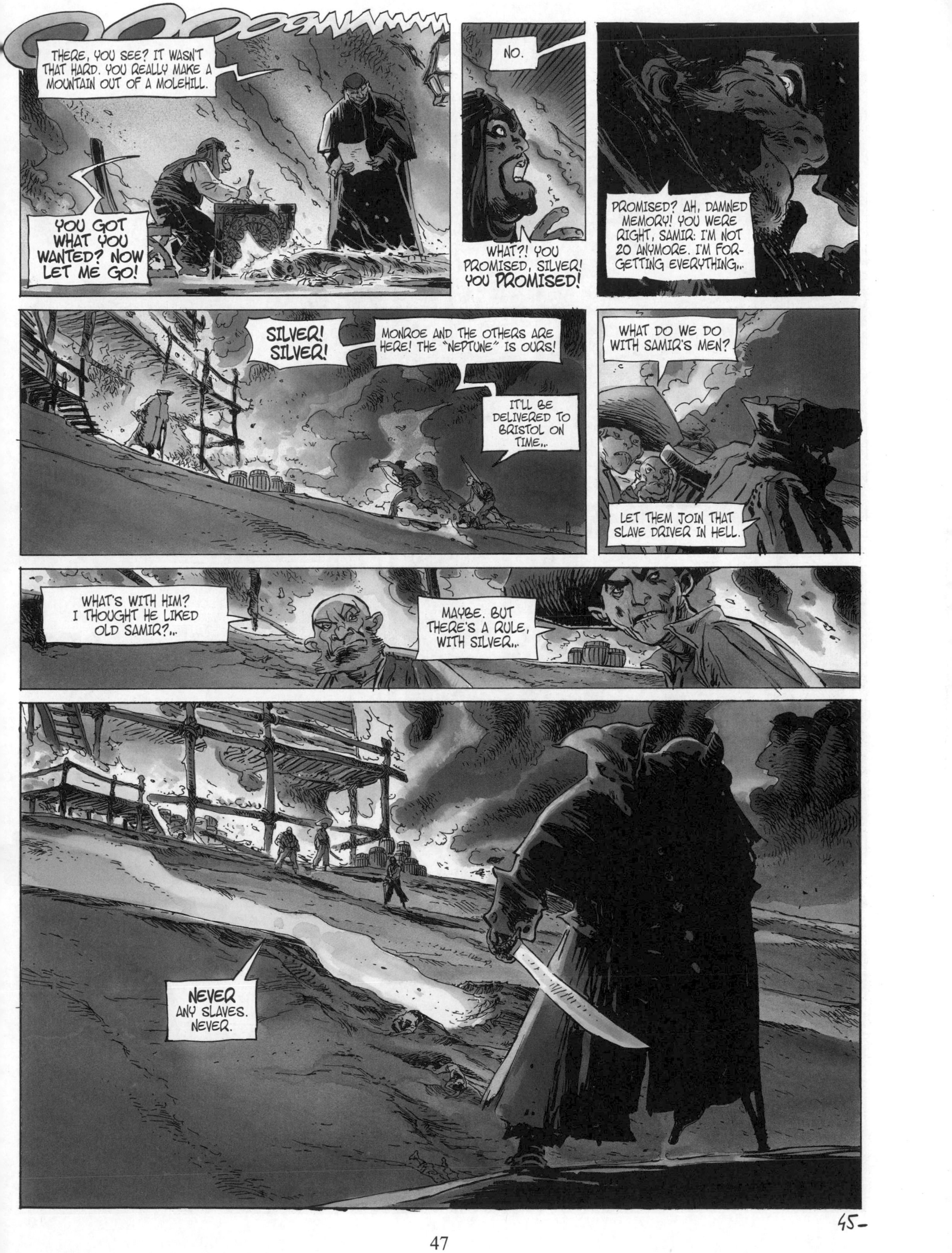
OOOOOOWAAAAAAAH
THERE, YOU SEE? IT WASN'T THAT HARD. YOU REALLY MAKE A MOUNTAIN OUT OF A MOLEHILL.
YOU GOT WHAT YOU WANTED? NOW LET ME GO!
NO.
WHAT?! YOU PROMISED, SILVER! YOU PROMISED!
PROMISED? AH, DAMNED MEMORY! YOU WERE RIGHT, SAMIR: I'M NOT 20 ANYMORE. I'M FORGETTING EVERYTHING...
SILVER! SILVER!
MONROE AND THE OTHERS ARE HERE! THE "NEPTUNE" IS OURS!
IT'LL BE DELIVERED TO BRISTOL ON TIME...
WHAT DO WE DO WITH SAMIR'S MEN?
LET THEM JOIN THAT SLAVE DRIVER IN HELL.
WHAT'S WITH HIM? I THOUGHT HE LIKED OLD SAMIR?...
MAYBE. BUT THERE'S A RULE, WITH SILVER...
NEVER ANY SLAVES. NEVER.
45-

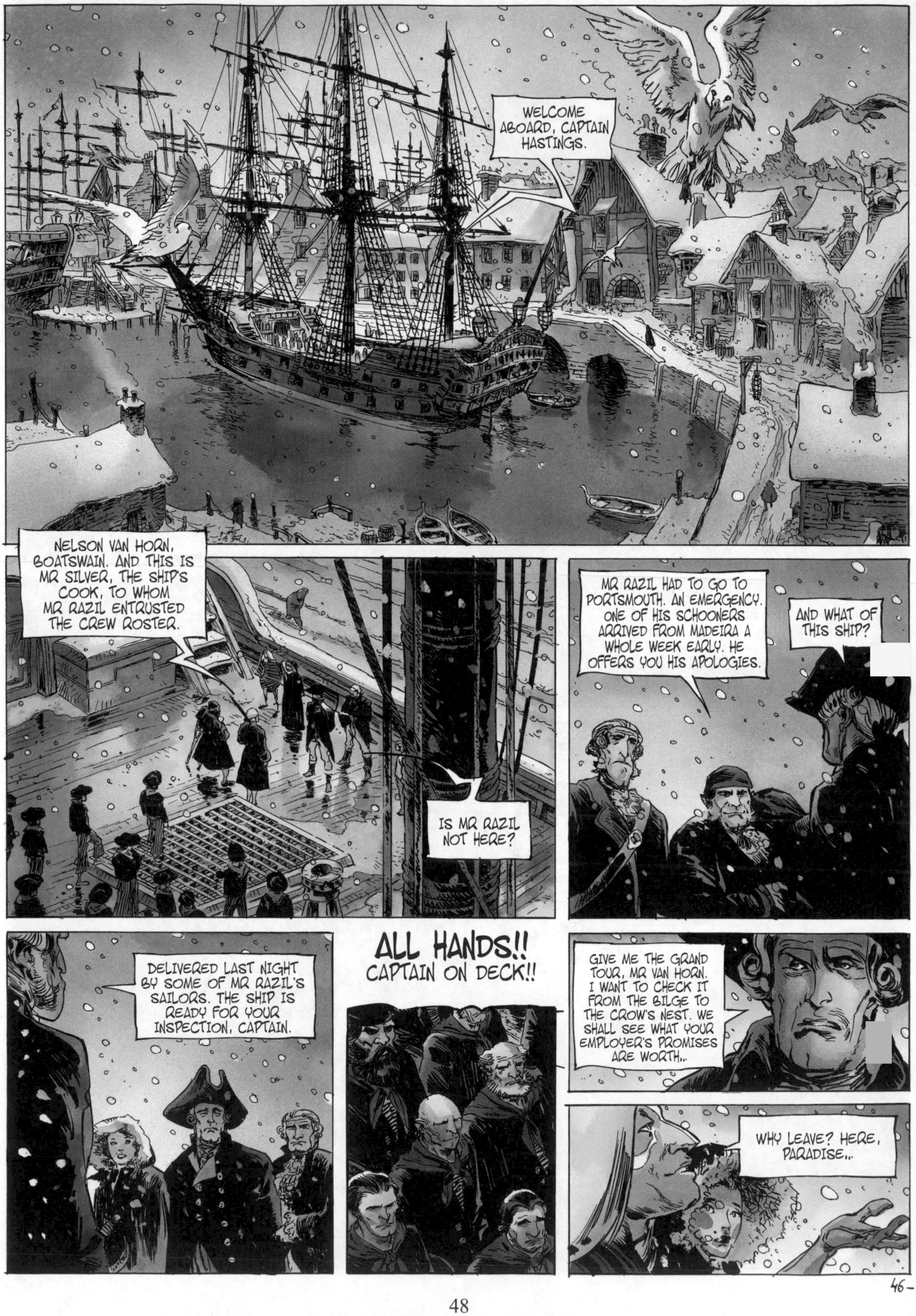
WELCOME ABOARD, CAPTAIN HASTINGS.
NELSON VAN HORN, BOATSWAIN. AND THIS IS MR SILVER, THE SHIP'S COOK, TO WHOM MR RAZIL ENTRUSTED THE CREW ROSTER.
IS MR RAZIL NOT HERE?
MR RAZIL HAD TO GO TO PORTSMOUTH. AN EMERGENCY. ONE OF HIS SCHOONERS ARRIVED FROM MADEIRA A WHOLE WEEK EARLY. HE OFFERS YOU HIS APOLOGIES.
AND WHAT OF THIS SHIP?
DELIVERED LAST NIGHT BY SOME OF MR RAZIL's SAILORS. THE SHIP IS READY FOR YOUR INSPECTION, CAPTAIN.
ALL HANDS!! CAPTAIN ON DECK!!
GIVE ME THE GRAND TOUR, MR VAN HORN. I WANT TO CHECK IT FROM THE BILGE TO THE CROW'S NEST. WE SHALL SEE WHAT YOUR EMPLOYER'S PROMISES ARE WORTH..
WHY LEAVE? HERE, PARADISE..

46–

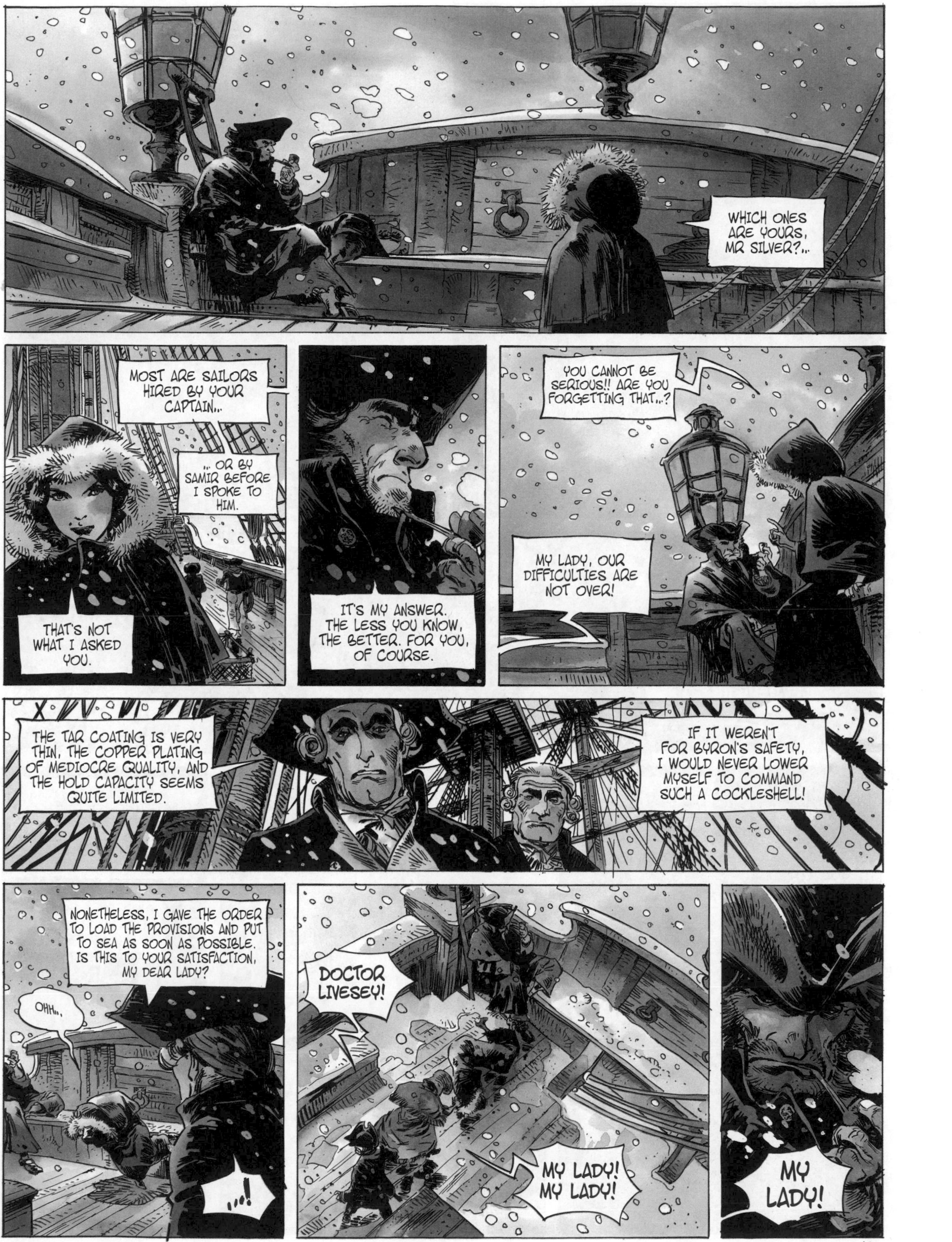
WHICH ONES ARE YOURS, MR SILVER?...
MOST ARE SAILORS HIRED BY YOUR CAPTAIN...
... OR BY SAMIR BEFORE I SPOKE TO HIM.
THAT'S NOT WHAT I ASKED YOU.
IT'S MY ANSWER. THE LESS YOU KNOW, THE BETTER. FOR YOU, OF COURSE.
YOU CANNOT BE SERIOUS!! ARE YOU FORGETTING THAT...?
MY LADY, OUR DIFFICULTIES ARE NOT OVER!
THE TAR COATING IS VERY THIN, THE COPPER PLATING OF MEDIOCRE QUALITY, AND THE HOLD CAPACITY SEEMS QUITE LIMITED.
IF IT WEREN'T FOR BYRON'S SAFETY, I WOULD NEVER LOWER MYSELF TO COMMAND SUCH A COCKLESHELL!
NONETHELESS, I GAVE THE ORDER TO LOAD THE PROVISIONS AND PUT TO SEA AS SOON AS POSSIBLE. IS THIS TO YOUR SATISFACTION, MY DEAR LADY?
OHH...
...!
DOCTOR LIVESEY!
MY LADY! MY LADY!
MY LADY!
47-

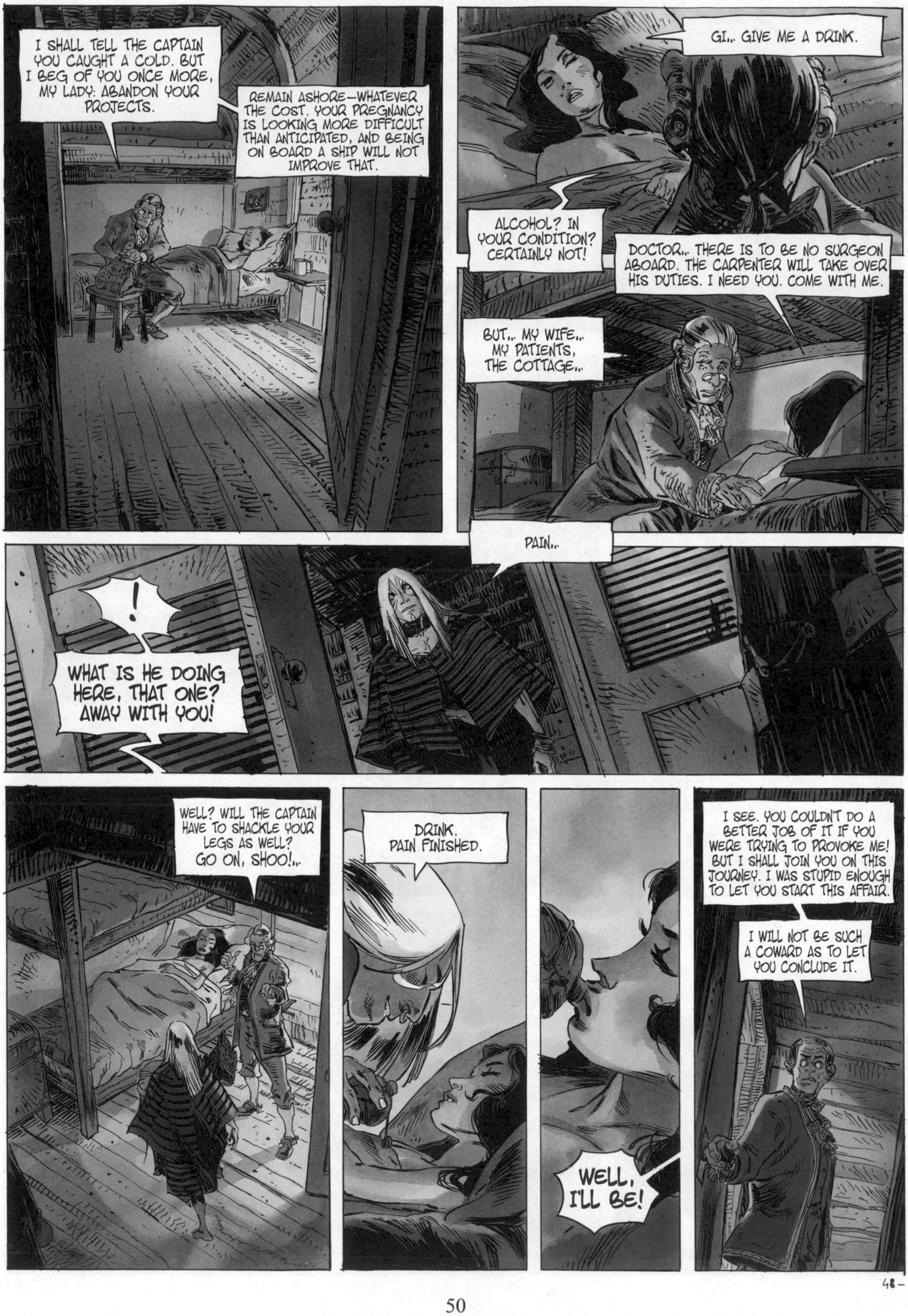
I SHALL TELL THE CAPTAIN YOU CAUGHT A COLD. BUT I BEG OF YOU ONCE MORE, MY LADY: ABANDON YOUR PROJECTS.
REMAIN ASHORE—WHATEVER THE COST. YOUR PREGNANCY IS LOOKING MORE DIFFICULT THAN ANTICIPATED, AND BEING ON BOARD A SHIP WILL NOT IMPROVE THAT.
GI... GIVE ME A DRINK.
ALCOHOL? IN YOUR CONDITION? CERTAINLY NOT!
DOCTOR... THERE IS TO BE NO SURGEON ABOARD. THE CARPENTER WILL TAKE OVER HIS DUTIES. I NEED YOU. COME WITH ME.
BUT... MY WIFE... MY PATIENTS, THE COTTAGE...
PAIN...
!
WHAT IS HE DOING HERE, THAT ONE? AWAY WITH YOU!
WELL? WILL THE CAPTAIN HAVE TO SHACKLE YOUR LEGS AS WELL? GO ON, SHOO!...
DRINK. PAIN FINISHED.
WELL, I'LL BE!
I SEE. YOU COULDN'T DO A BETTER JOB OF IT IF YOU WERE TRYING TO PROVOKE ME! BUT I SHALL JOIN YOU ON THIS JOURNEY. I WAS STUPID ENOUGH TO LET YOU START THIS AFFAIR.
I WILL NOT BE SUCH A COWARD AS TO LET YOU CONCLUDE IT.
48–

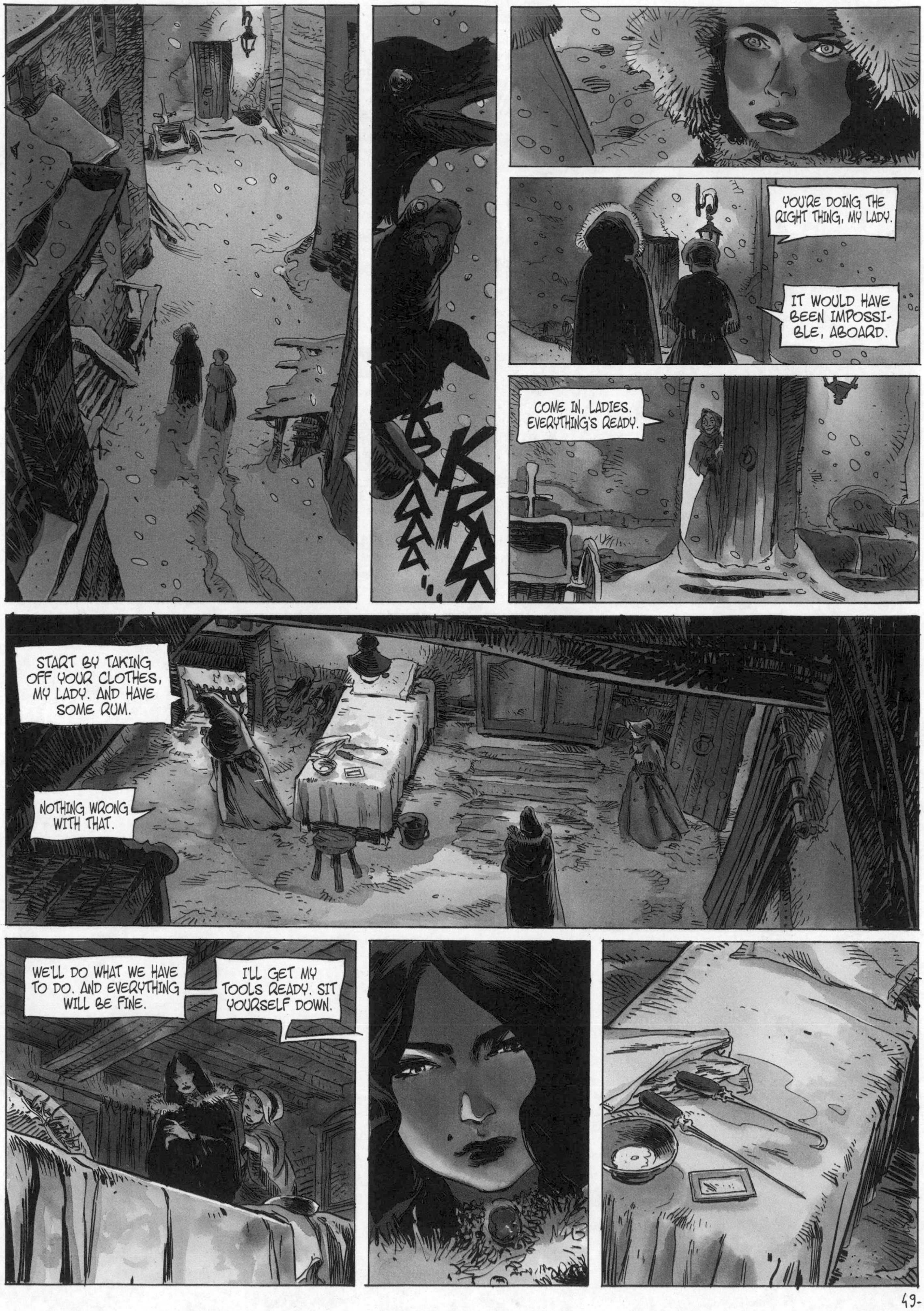
SKRAAAA...
YOU'RE DOING THE RIGHT THING, MY LADY.
IT WOULD HAVE BEEN IMPOSSI-BLE, ABOARD.
COME IN, LADIES. EVERYTHING'S READY.
START BY TAKING OFF YOUR CLOTHES, MY LADY. AND HAVE SOME RUM.
NOTHING WRONG WITH THAT.
WE'LL DO WHAT WE HAVE TO DO. AND EVERYTHING WILL BE FINE.
I'LL GET MY TOOLS READY. SIT YOURSELF DOWN.
49-

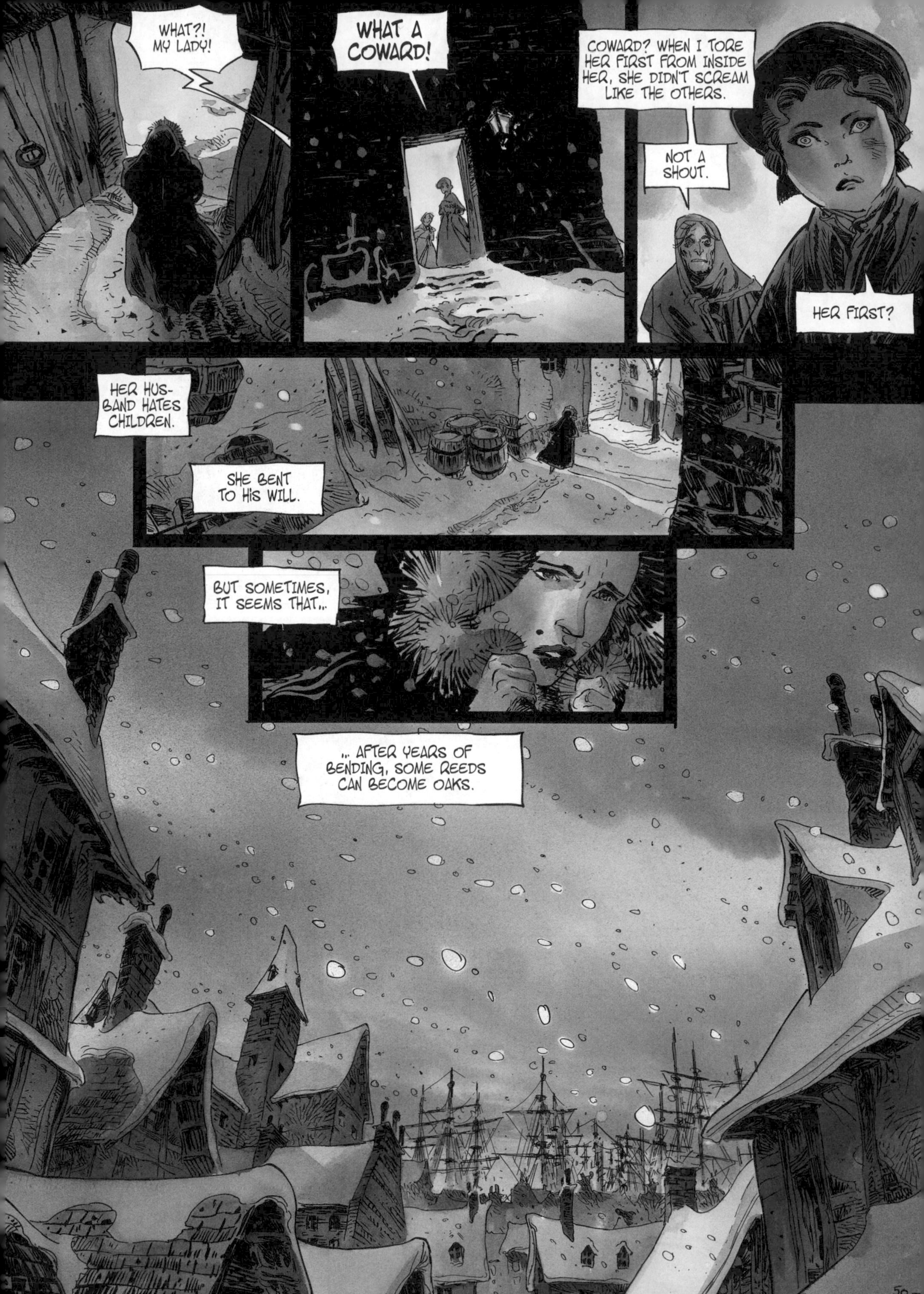
WHAT?! MY LADY!
WHAT A COWARD!
COWARD? WHEN I TORE HER FIRST FROM INSIDE HER, SHE DIDN'T SCREAM LIKE THE OTHERS.
NOT A SHOUT.
HER FIRST?
HER HUS-BAND HATES CHILDREN.
SHE BENT TO HIS WILL.
BUT SOMETIMES, IT SEEMS THAT...
... AFTER YEARS OF BENDING, SOME REEDS CAN BECOME OAKS.

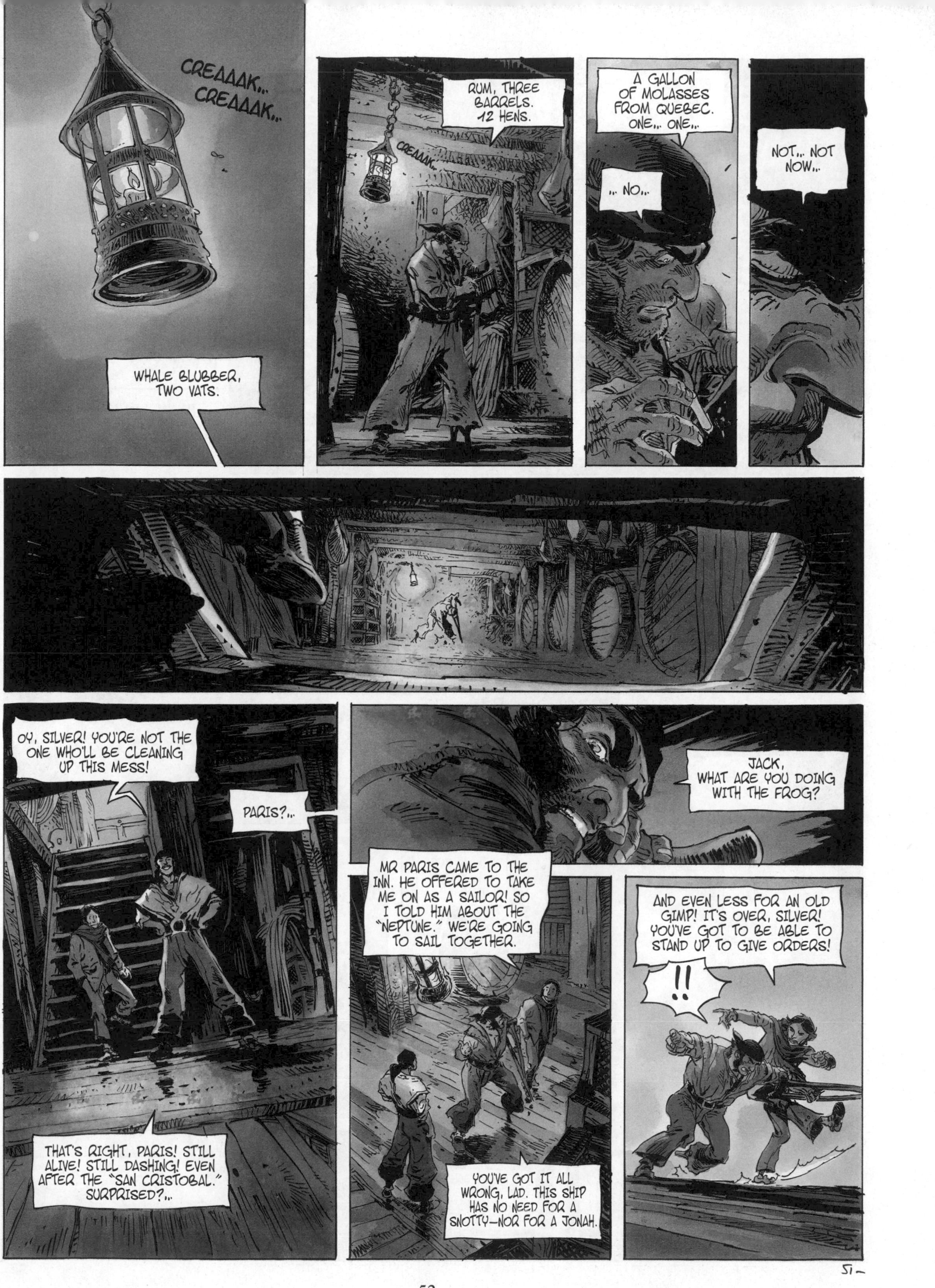
CREAAAK... CREAAAK...
WHALE BLUBBER, TWO VATS.
RUM, THREE BARRELS. 12 HENS.
CREAAAK...
A GALLON OF MOLASSES FROM QUEBEC. ONE... ONE...
... NO...
NOT... NOT NOW...
OY, SILVER! YOU'RE NOT THE ONE WHO'LL BE CLEANING UP THIS MESS!
PARIS?...
THAT'S RIGHT, PARIS! STILL ALIVE! STILL DASHING! EVEN AFTER THE "SAN CRISTOBAL." SURPRISED?...
JACK, WHAT ARE YOU DOING WITH THE FROG?
MR PARIS CAME TO THE INN. HE OFFERED TO TAKE ME ON AS A SAILOR! SO I TOLD HIM ABOUT THE "NEPTUNE." WE'RE GOING TO SAIL TOGETHER.
YOU'VE GOT IT ALL WRONG, LAD. THIS SHIP HAS NO NEED FOR A SNOTTY—NOR FOR A JONAH.
AND EVEN LESS FOR AN OLD GIMP! IT'S OVER, SILVER! YOU'VE GOT TO BE ABLE TO STAND UP TO GIVE ORDERS!
!!

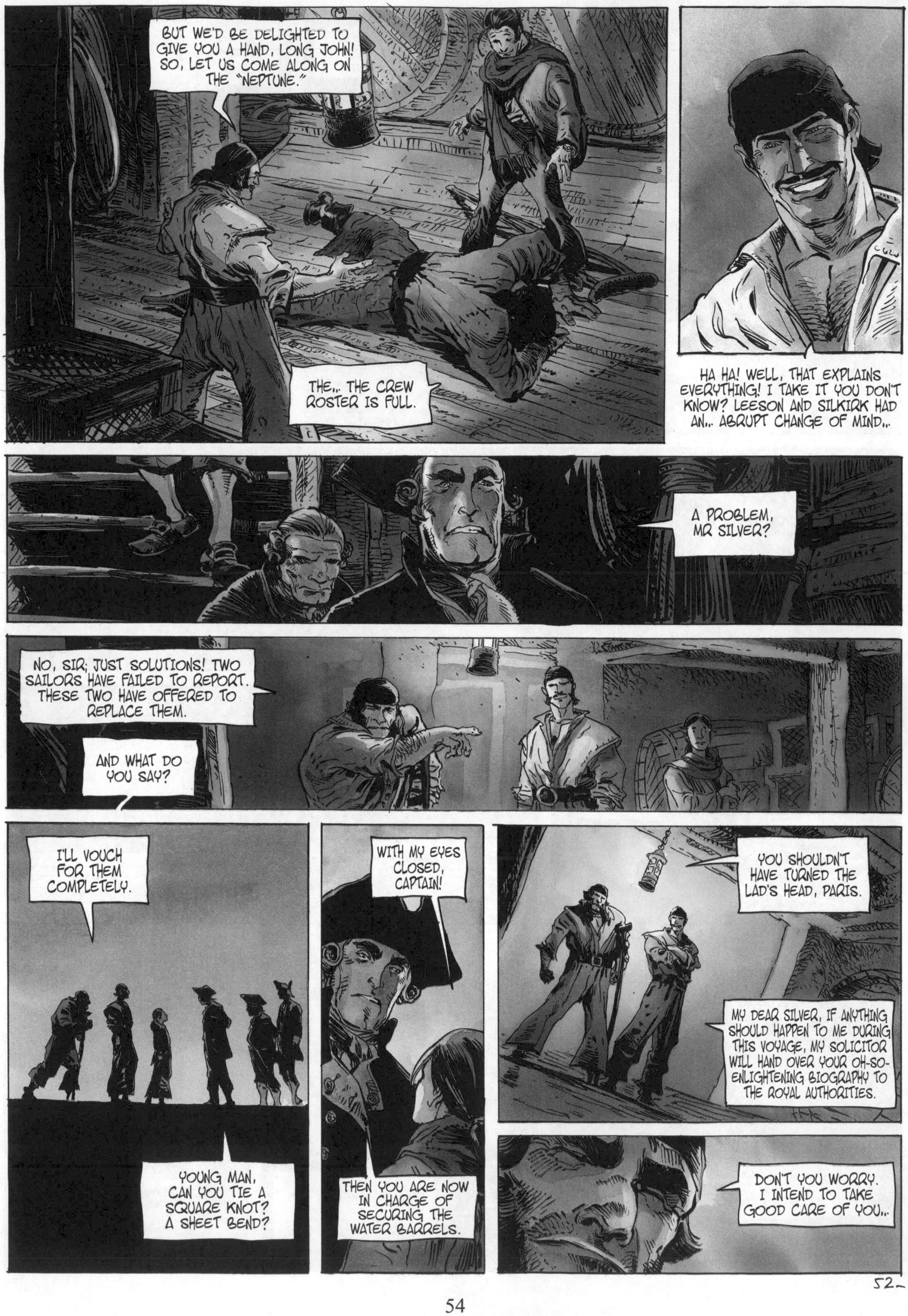
BUT WE'D BE DELIGHTED TO GIVE YOU A HAND, LONG JOHN! SO, LET US COME ALONG ON THE "NEPTUNE."
THE... THE CREW ROSTER IS FULL.
HA HA! WELL, THAT EXPLAINS EVERYTHING! I TAKE IT YOU DON'T KNOW? LEESON AND SILKIRK HAD AN... ABRUPT CHANGE OF MIND...
A PROBLEM, MR SILVER?
NO, SIR; JUST SOLUTIONS! TWO SAILORS HAVE FAILED TO REPORT. THESE TWO HAVE OFFERED TO REPLACE THEM.
AND WHAT DO YOU SAY?
I'LL VOUCH FOR THEM COMPLETELY.
YOUNG MAN, CAN YOU TIE A SQUARE KNOT? A SHEET BEND?
WITH MY EYES CLOSED, CAPTAIN!
THEN YOU ARE NOW IN CHARGE OF SECURING THE WATER BARRELS.
YOU SHOULDN'T HAVE TURNED THE LAD'S HEAD, PARIS.
MY DEAR SILVER, IF ANYTHING SHOULD HAPPEN TO ME DURING THIS VOYAGE, MY SOLICITOR WILL HAND OVER YOUR OH-SO-ENLIGHTENING BIOGRAPHY TO THE ROYAL AUTHORITIES.
DON'T YOU WORRY. I INTEND TO TAKE GOOD CARE OF YOU...
52

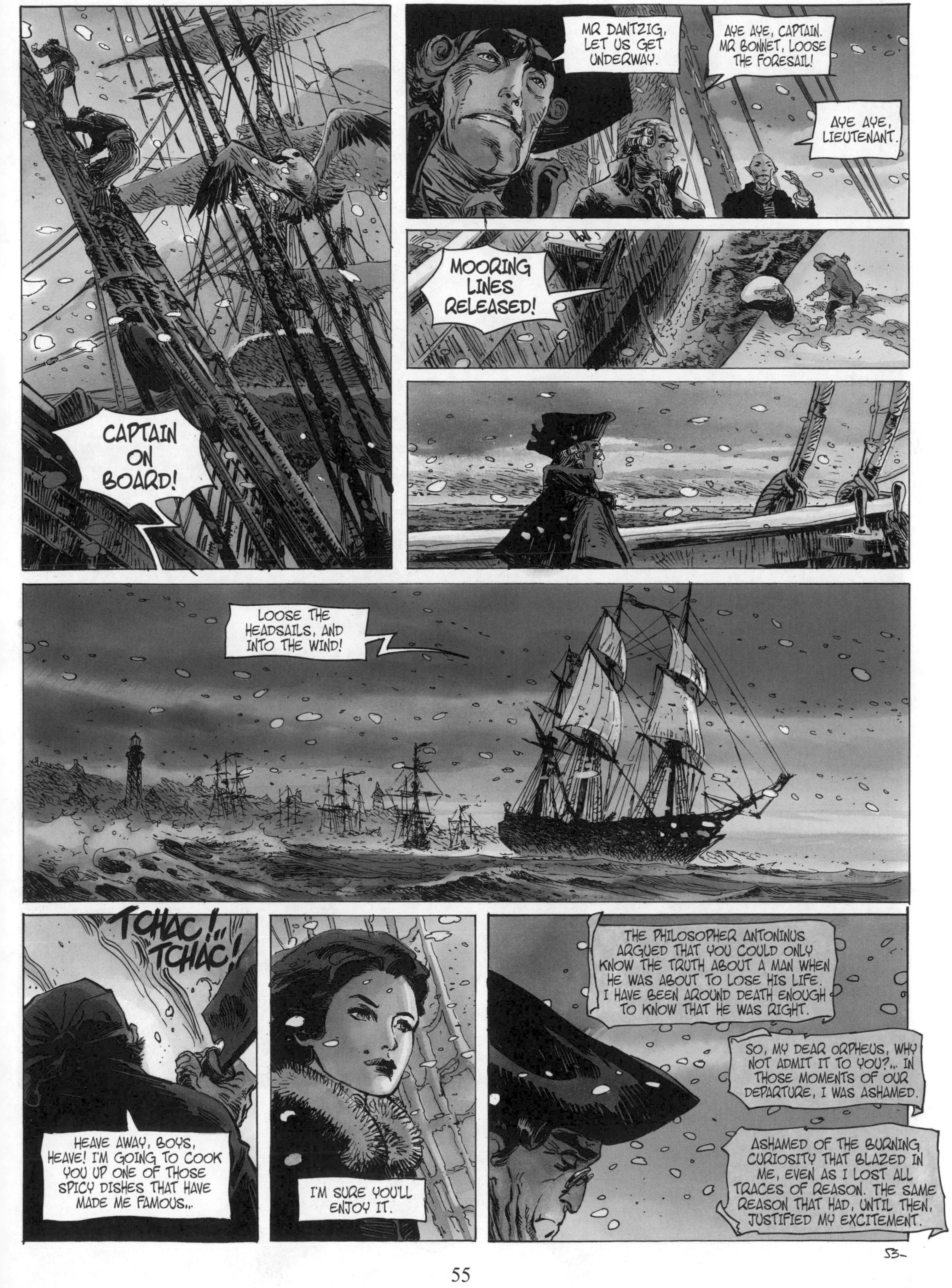
CAPTAIN ON BOARD!
MR DANTZIG, LET US GET UNDERWAY.
AYE AYE, CAPTAIN. MR BONNET, LOOSE THE FORESAIL!
AYE AYE, LIEUTENANT.
MOORING LINES RELEASED!
LOOSE THE HEADSAILS, AND INTO THE WIND!
TCHAC!.. TCHAC!
HEAVE AWAY, BOYS, HEAVE! I'M GOING TO COOK YOU UP ONE OF THOSE SPICY DISHES THAT HAVE MADE ME FAMOUS...
I'M SURE YOU'LL ENJOY IT.
THE PHILOSOPHER ANTONINUS ARGUED THAT YOU COULD ONLY KNOW THE TRUTH ABOUT A MAN WHEN HE WAS ABOUT TO LOSE HIS LIFE. I HAVE BEEN AROUND DEATH ENOUGH TO KNOW THAT HE WAS RIGHT.
SO, MY DEAR ORPHEUS, WHY NOT ADMIT IT TO YOU?.. IN THOSE MOMENTS OF OUR DEPARTURE, I WAS ASHAMED.
ASHAMED OF THE BURNING CURIOSITY THAT BLAZED IN ME, EVEN AS I LOST ALL TRACES OF REASON. THE SAME REASON THAT HAD, UNTIL THEN, JUSTIFIED MY EXCITEMENT.

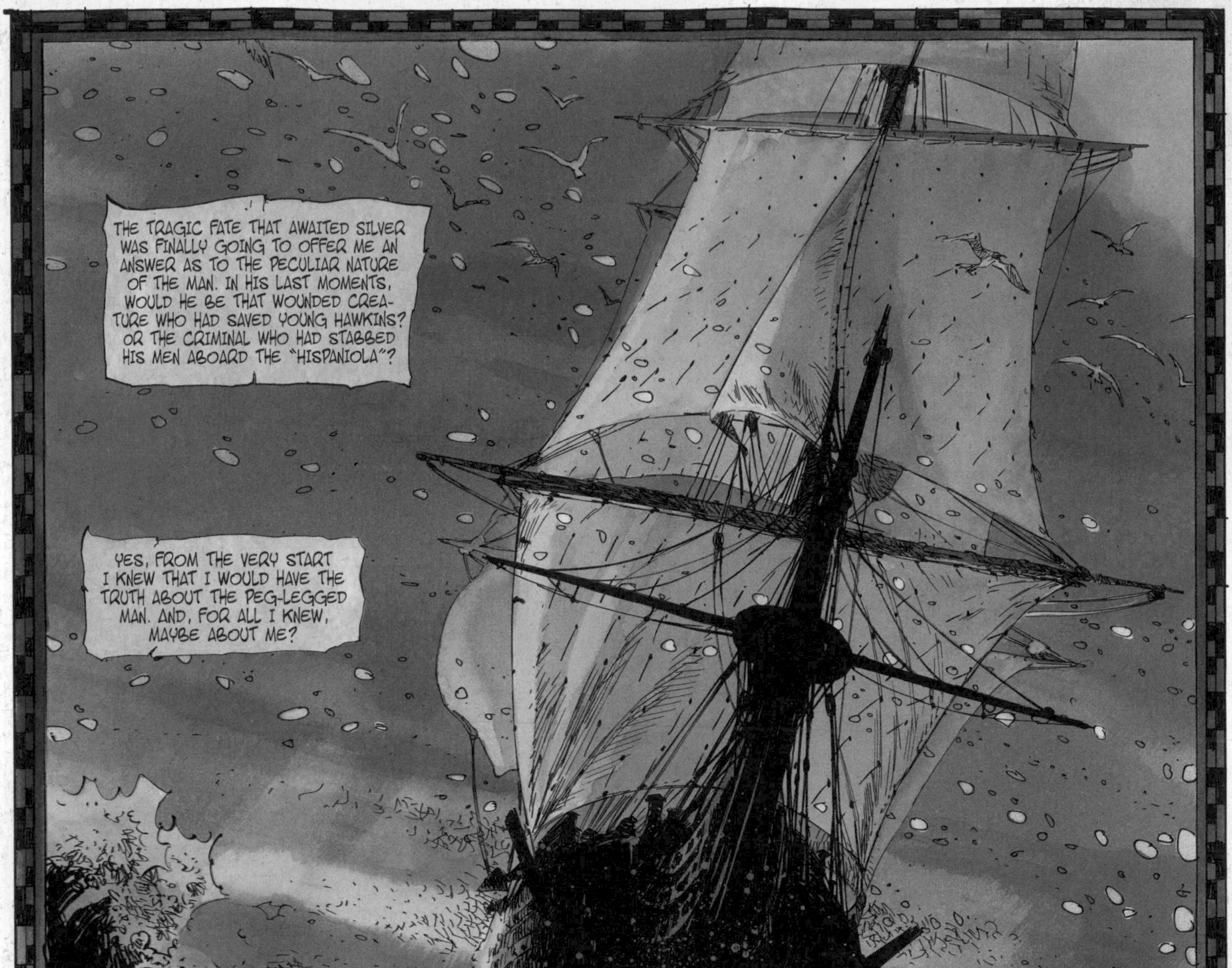
THE TRAGIC FATE THAT AWAITED SILVER WAS FINALLY GOING TO OFFER ME AN ANSWER AS TO THE PECULIAR NATURE OF THE MAN. IN HIS LAST MOMENTS, WOULD HE BE THAT WOUNDED CREATURE WHO HAD SAVED YOUNG HAWKINS? OR THE CRIMINAL WHO HAD STABBED HIS MEN ABOARD THE "HISPANIOLA"?
YES, FROM THE VERY START I KNEW THAT I WOULD HAVE THE TRUTH ABOUT THE PEG-LEGGED MAN. AND, FOR ALL I KNEW, MAYBE ABOUT ME?
AFTER ALL, WHO COULD HAVE PREDICTED HOW MANY OF US WOULD EVER SEE ENGLAND AGAIN?...
54

DORISON - LAUFFRAY 2006 LONG JOHN SILVER I TO BE CONTINUED...

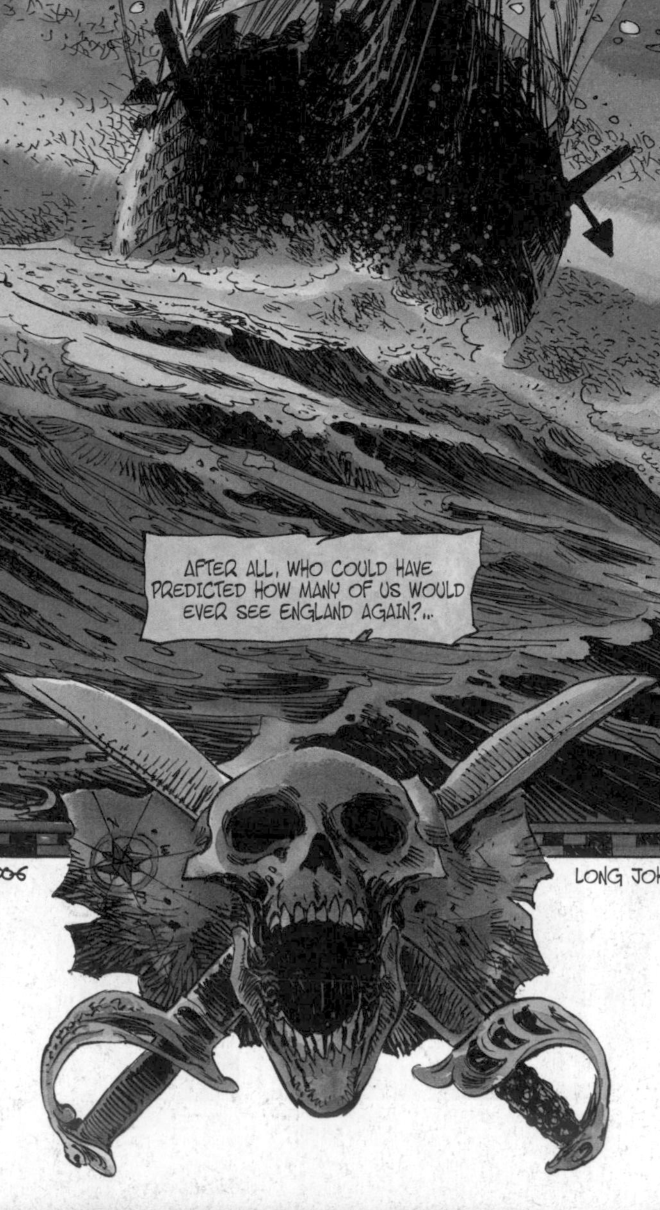